KU-765-872

Contents

Introduction

STUDENT LIFE is Volume 333 in the **ISSUES** series. The aim of the series is to offer current, diverse information about important issues in our world, from a UK perspective.

ABOUT STUDENT LIFE

Deciding what to do after you finish your A-levels is a big decision. You might be asking yourself, "do I enter the world of work with an apprenticeship, or should I go to university?" This book explores the options open to students and considers the issues such as financial hardship and stress suffered by some students. It also considers the benefits offered by both university life and apprenticeships.

OUR SOURCES

Titles in the **ISSUES** series are designed to function as educational resource books, providing a balanced overview of a specific subject.

The information in our books is comprised of facts, articles and opinions from many different sources, including:

⇨ Newspaper reports and opinion pieces

⇨ Website factsheets

⇨ Magazine and journal articles

⇨ Statistics and surveys

⇨ Government reports

⇨ Literature from special interest groups.

A NOTE ON CRITICAL EVALUATION

Because the information reprinted here is from a number of different sources, readers should bear in mind the origin of the text and whether the source is likely to have a particular bias when presenting information (or when conducting their research). It is hoped that, as you read about the many aspects of the issues explored in this book, you will critically evaluate the information presented.

It is important that you decide whether you are being presented with facts or opinions. Does the writer give a biased or unbiased report? If an opinion is being expressed, do you agree with the writer? Is there potential bias to the 'facts' or statistics behind an article?

ASSIGNMENTS

In the back of this book, you will find a selection of assignments designed to help you engage with the articles you have been reading and to explore your own opinions. Some tasks will take longer than others and there is a mixture of design, writing and research-based activities that you can complete alone or in a group.

Useful weblinks

www.bbench.co.uk

www.theconversation.com

www.ditchthelabel.org

www.elevationnetworks.org

www.fullfact.org

www.theguardian.com

www.huffingtonpost.co.uk

www.ifs.org.uk

www.independent.co.uk

www.mind.org.uk

www.nus.org.uk

www.ons.gov.uk

www.researchbriefings.parliament.uk

www.surrey.ac.uk

FURTHER RESEARCH

At the end of each article we have listed its source and a website that you can visit if you would like to conduct your own research. Please remember to critically evaluate any sources that you consult and consider whether the information you are viewing is accurate and unbiased.

Here's what to do if you're disappointed with your A-level results

THE CONVERSATION

An article from The Conversation.

By Myfanwy Bugler, Lecturer of Psychology, University of Hull

The saying goes "what doesn't kill you makes you stronger", and while that may well be the case, you still need to have the right mindset to turn failure into success – especially on exam results day.

This means rather than being overwhelmed by a challenge, you need to find a way to overcome it and learn from the experience so you can succeed in the future. This builds what psychologists call "mental toughness", which basically means that you are able to deal with challenges, pressure and competition, irrespective of prevailing circumstances.

People with mental toughness bounce back after a disappointment and see failure as a challenge and a learning opportunity, rather than a setback. The good news is mental toughness can be learned through experience, so there's no better time to start than on exam results day – when mental toughness will help you get through the day and help you to assess your future options if you haven't done as well as you expected.

Time for self-reflection

You first need to reflect on why you missed the grades. Look at what went wrong and how you might learn from that. Think about Mo Farah in the Olympics 10,000-metre final. He fell badly and it could have cost him the gold medal. But he got back up, put it behind him and carried on – eventually winning the race.

Don't dwell on the 'failure'. Work out what went wrong, put it to one side, and then start to look forwards.

It's good to talk

However, the worst thing you can do is sweep a bad result under the carpet. Once you've worked out where you think you went wrong, it's important to discuss what's happened and why.

It's natural to feel nervous about the future, especially if things haven't quite worked out how you imagined, and chatting these thoughts and fears through with someone close to you can really help to take some of the weight off your mind.

Parents, this is where you can step in and encourage your child to open up and let them know you are still there for them.

Don't be overwhelmed by emotion

It's hard not to panic when your social media feeds are full of excited friends off to their first choice of uni. Results day is a big deal, but wallowing in emotion will affect your ability to make all those important decisions yet to come.

Speak to sensible people around you for practical advice and try to think positively. It might feel like everything rests on your grades but actually many universities look at the whole person.

But don't trivialise

This might be the first major failure you've experienced and with emotions running high it is easy to feel like this is the end of the world. Parents can help here by remembering the importance of taking the experience seriously without making things worse.

At this point it might be good to talk about how far you've come and how much there is still left to achieve. Not only is this good for confidence all round, but it could also help formulate some interview answers when you speak to universities.

Work out your strengths

Think about other achievements which show commitment and success, such as playing an instrument, being in a sports team, having a part-time job. Write them down and use them when you speak to universities.

If you'd been predicted high grades but were crippled by nerves on exam day, you've obviously got some academic ability and exams only provide a snapshot. Figure out what your strengths are and what makes you stand out against your peers.

Think outside the box

You may feel helpless but it's important to use your time wisely and try and figure out some alternative options. If you've fixated on one particular university, does it offer other courses, or is there another university which has a similar feel?

If it's all about the course, where else offers that programme or can you explore alternative routes like foundation degrees? The process of school, exams and results can feel like a treadmill and clearing can be an opportunity to step off and change direction.

Do lunch …

Or dinner, or a film. Don't stew at home alone all day as your friends post happy pictures on social media. Plan something low key but positive for the day like a meal at a favourite restaurant with your family – that way you can still have a nice time regardless of the results.

This will also give you a chance to take your mind off things and unwind a bit after the stress of the last few days.

Realise how far you've come

If you're struggling to get past your disappointment, think back to when you were doing your GCSEs – maybe even read an essay you wrote back then. See how far you have come. I get my students to keep one of their first-year essays then re-read it in class in their final year. They cannot believe how much they've improved.

Your A-levels are a big leap from GCSEs and your degree is another step further. As hard as it feels now, once you are at university and having an amazing time this day won't feel nearly as painful. Just make sure you learn from the experience and build that mental toughness.

18 August 2016

⇨ The above information is reprinted with kind permission from *The Conversation*. Please visit www.theconversation.com for further information.

Here are the best cities for British students to study in

By Alex Jackson, The Huffington Post UK

Students get ready to pack your bags and jet off across Europe.

Berlin has been named as the top European university city for British students abroad, along with a shortlist featuring many other popular European destinations.

Germany, which largely offers free tuition to students from EU member countries, has ranked top after an analysis of the cost of living, the quality of education, tuition fees and the English-taught courses available to study.

The survey, which was organised by TransferWise, the online international banking service, is supposed to help British students make a more informed choice about where they choose to study in Europe.

Unveiling the figures, TransferWise said: "We realised students in the UK are simply unaware of the opportunities available to them in Europe, so we thought we'd help them find out what's on offer."

The number of students opting for courses abroad has risen significantly in recent years, due to the increase in student fees in the UK. These 'tuition fee refugees' are escaping from the highest tuition fees in the world, with average charges of £6,000 per year making UK universities more expensive than comparable institutions in Australia and the US.

Berlin came out on top thanks to its enticing nightlife, efficient and effective transport and its varied culture scene.

11 February 2016

⇨ The above information is reprinted with kind permission from The Huffington Post UK. Please visit www.huffingtonpost.co.uk for further information.

Should I go to university or do an apprenticeship?

Deciding what to do after you finish your A-levels is a big decision. You might be asking yourself, "do I enter the world of work with an apprenticeship, or should I go to university?"

The degree versus apprenticeship debate is long-running and choosing your next educational move requires careful consideration. Higher education continues to be a popular option despite the rise in tuition fees, with an all-time high of 241,585 18-year-olds across the UK accepted onto degree courses in 2017.

However, attitudes to apprenticeships have also evolved and they are now recognised as an equal alternative to university. Since 2014, 56,200 workers have enrolled on higher and degree apprenticeships, studying a range of qualifications from foundation degree level to full Masters.

The main benefits of each option can be summarised as follows:

⇨ Going to university – you'll be able to pick from thousands of courses, a degree will leave your career more open-ended in terms of future opportunities and you'll acquire a whole range of soft skills, transferrable to any job role.

⇨ Doing an apprenticeship – you'll be gaining valuable on-the-job experience and earning money as you study. You'll also be exempt from paying tuition fees.

Here we weigh up the benefits of each option in more detail to help make a tricky decision that little bit easier. If you're still unsure, be comforted by the fact that it isn't a case of choosing university or apprenticeship – it's possible to do both.

What subjects are on offer?

If you choose to study at university you'll be able to pick from thousands of courses. This variety can be useful if you're unsure of what to do after graduation as you can opt for a broader subject and keep your options open.

You might also be surprised at the scope of apprenticeships on offer. They are no longer dominated by the manual trades and the engineering sector, and instead span a range of industries including accountancy, IT, law, media, publishing and journalism. Soon you'll have even more choice, as the Government has pledged to create a further three million apprenticeships by 2020.

What will I learn?

Although vocational degrees are on the rise, university study is primarily focused on education and research. Following a theory-based approach you'll learn about your subject through lectures, seminars and workshops, and graduate with a Bachelors degree. You'll then head out into the world of work to test your knowledge and put into practice what you've learned.

Apprenticeships appeal to those looking for alternatives to university as they take a more practical approach to learning. You'll focus on training for a specific career and learn your trade by actually doing the job.

You'll gain hands-on experience and have the opportunity to apply your skills immediately. On completion you could hold an NVQ, HNC or HND, while higher apprenticeships can lead to a foundation degree and degree, apprenticeships and work experience can result in a full honours degree.

What job opportunities are available?

A university education allows you to target a broader range of careers than you can through an apprenticeship, but both will stand you in good stead when it comes to looking for a job.

Apprenticeships are restrictive in the sense that the training and skills that you gain are specific to a particular industry or role. However, if you're confident in your career choice you'll be well equipped to take advantage of apprenticeship opportunities.

Bear in mind that, in sectors such as healthcare, business and science, you'll need a degree to enter certain professions. These professions include:

⇨ ecologist

⇨ hospital doctor

⇨ nanotechnologist

⇨ psychotherapist

⇨ psychiatrist

⇨ surgeon.

Other sectors benefit from the practical, on-the-job training that higher and degree apprenticeships provide, such as roles in engineering and manufacturing and work experience, property and construction and the media.

How much will it cost?

Apprenticeships undoubtedly win this round. If you're under 25 the Government and your employer fund your training so you don't have to pay a penny.

On the other hand, studying for a degree will cost you £9,000 per year in tuition fees, plus additional living expenses. It's estimated that an undergraduate could leave university with up to £50,000 worth of debt. However you won't start repayments until you earn a minimum of £21,000 a year.

What will I earn?

If you opt for university you'll have to wait until after graduation to start earning a full-time wage. As an apprentice you'll earn while you learn and receive the national minimum wage for apprentices. If you're aged between 16 and 18 the rate currently stands at £3.30. This rate also applies to those aged 19 or over who are currently in their first year of training.

The earning potential of university graduates and apprentices has been examined in recent research by The Sutton Trust, which found that top apprentices can expect to earn thousands more in their lifetime than undergraduates from a non-Russell Group university.

In fact, those who opt to study for a level 5 higher apprenticeship will earn £1.5 million during the course of their career, almost £52,000 more than graduates from non-elite universities who can expect to earn £1.4 million. However, students from top Russell Group universities come out on top with estimated lifetime earnings of £1.6 million.

What do employers think?

Both methods of study are highly regarded by employers. University is respected for the depth of knowledge and transferrable skills it provides, while apprenticeships are valued for their practical nature and real-life work experience opportunities.

More organisations than ever before are offering apprenticeship schemes as employers come to view this method of training as a viable alternative to a university degree. However, educated graduates are in high demand and look set to remain so for the foreseeable future.

If you have ambitions to work for a particular company it might be helpful to find out what they look for in a candidate, which do they value most, qualifications or experience? This could help when making your decision.

It's a tough choice to make and one option isn't necessarily better than the other. Take a look at your current

Case Study: Apprentice – Edward Thomson

An ambition to work in the building trade led Edward to apply for an apprenticeship with construction company Redrow. He's now heading to university to become a quantity surveyor

What qualifications do you have?

I have two A-levels in law and psychology and GCSEs in all the relevant subjects with grades ranging from A to C.

I also now hold a BTEC Level 3 in Construction in the Built Environment and an Edexcel Level 3 NVQ Diploma in Surveying, Property and Maintenance.

Why did you decide to do an apprenticeship?

I've always wanted to work in the building trade. I applied for a number of apprenticeships after leaving school – to no avail. After hearing about the opportunity at Redrow I decided to apply one last time. I secured an interview and was then offered the job.

How did you find and apply for your apprenticeship?

I learned about the apprenticeship through a family member who works for the Construction Industry Training Board (CITB). I sent my CV in to Redrow who held it on file for a couple of months and then entered it into the application process.

How does the apprenticeship work?

The apprenticeship lasted two years and during this time I worked full time with six "block" weeks set aside for training for the BTEC qualification. Each training week would cover a different aspect of the apprenticeship. For example, the first week would be maths, the second would be measurement, the third would be tendering, etc.

As an apprentice, my responsibilities covered all aspects of quantity surveying work including tendering, payments, visiting sites, valuations and negotiating, etc.

What did you enjoy about your apprenticeship?

I enjoyed watching a site turn from a derelict wasteland into a respectable housing estate. It was also interesting to see how all the work comes together and to discover what can go wrong when working on a project.

What did you find the most challenging?

Apart from the early mornings, the array of information that I had to absorb on a daily basis was a challenge. You need knowledge of lots of building trades and you then need to know how each trade links in with another. It's a huge learning curve that keeps getting bigger as you aim to fill the gaps in your knowledge.

What are your plans for after your apprenticeship?

I have ambitions to become a fully-qualified quantity surveyor. I plan to start university in September so I'll go from there.

What advice would give to others?

An apprenticeship is a fool-proof way of gaining qualifications and knowledge while getting paid to do a job. A good quality apprenticeship is worth every second of your time and can even fund your aspirations of university study.

The best advice I can give to anyone working towards an apprenticeship is to stick at it, after a few years, who knows where it will lead?

Case Study: Apprentice – Luke Johnson

A keen interest in technology prompted Luke to apply for a BT technical networking apprenticeship. Find out what he enjoys about his role...

How did you find and apply for your apprenticeship?

I found an advert for this particular apprenticeship in a local newspaper and applied online. I then got through to an assessment centre at Adastral Park, BT's Global Research and Development Headquarters.

Why did you decide to do an apprenticeship?

I have a keen interest in technology which prompted me to start looking around after I failed to get into medical school.

I considered taking a gap year and applying again but was really intrigued as to what BT could offer, especially as they were launching BT Sport at the time – football is a particular passion of mine.

How does the apprenticeship work?

I am currently completing a three-year higher apprenticeship in a technical networking role. During this time I'll receive a sponsored foundation degree at University Campus Suffolk (UCS), a level 4 NVQ and also build up lots of on-the-job training and experience, which is invaluable in today's job market.

With an apprenticeship you get the best of both worlds and come out the other side work-ready and qualified.

What do you enjoy about your apprenticeship?

I love all of the opportunities and extras I've been able to get involved with. The chance to make a significant and positive impact on the company and those you volunteer for is such a fulfilling feeling and something that I want to carry on for the rest of my BT career.

The highlight of my apprenticeship has been a careers evening solely arranged by my #SPARKanInterest Challenge Cup team, which was an incredible success. The feedback we received from both BT and the guests who attended was amazing.

Knowing we have had a positive impact on someone's life, as well as helping the business to engage with lots more students was very uplifting.

What has been the most challenging part?

Completing a foundation degree and NVQ alongside my day-job, which includes project work, can be quite intensive but challenges are a huge part of a BT apprenticeship.

What are your plans for the future?

I want to complete the top-up course to get a full degree and I'd then love to work in a role that keeps me deeply involved with the school engagement and apprenticeship framework.

What advice would you give others who are planning to do an apprenticeship?

Do the legwork and show initiative – get work experience, attend events held by the recruiting company and make them aware of you before you even apply. A lot can be said for setting a great first impression.

situation – consider what qualifications you already hold, what you'd like to study, your finances and what you'd like to do in the future. Do some research and choose the best option for you.

You could work towards an apprenticeship and then go to university or similarly get a degree and then do an apprenticeship. However, if you pick the latter course of action, the same apprenticeship funding might not be available.

7 March 2018

⇨ The above information is reprinted with kind permission from National Union of Students. Please visit www. nus. org.uk for further information.

Bristol University gives a third of scholarships for 'disadvantaged' teens to private school pupils

A quarter of children in the city live in poverty.

By Jasmin Gray

A top university has faced harsh criticism after it was revealed it gave a third of scholarships aimed at disadvantaged local teenagers to private school pupils.

In December, the University of Bristol announced it would lower entry requirements for some students in a bid to improve social mobility, giving priority to young carers, teens in care and those who receive free school meals, among others.

"We want to recruit the most able students, regardless of their background," Vice Chancellor Professor Hugh Brady said at the time.

But figures obtained by student newspaper *Epigram* have shown that 33% of these adjusted offers – based on potential and progress rather than grades – have been made to private school students.

With 14% of sixth-formers nationally attending private schools, critics claim that independent school pupils are overrepresented on the scheme.

The university has defended its decision, saying these pupils fulfil the "widening participation criteria".

The 93% Club, the university's state school society, told the paper it "lamented" the fact that independent schools have been included in the Bristol Scholars programme.

"Students from state-funded schools will by and large not have the same opportunities that those from independent schools enjoy," a spokesperson said.

"It would therefore not make sense to include those who already have had the privilege of a private education, at the expense of state school students

who would better benefit from the opportunity."

One in four children in Bristol currently live in poverty.

As part the innovative social mobility scheme, Bristol University vowed to offer five pupils with "high potential" from every school and college in the city a guaranteed place to study the course of their choice.

But some teachers and organisations have defended the scheme, suggesting that need is not always due to poverty.

Lucy Collins, head of UK recruitment at Bristol University, said: "Bristol Scholars from independent schools who have been offered places had to fulfil one or more widening participation criteria in order to be selected. For example, they

may have faced a disrupted education due to ill health or family difficulties.

"At the heart of the Bristol Scholars scheme is the determination to provide opportunities for local students whose potential is not recognised in their predicted A-Level results."

2 March 2017

⇨ The above information is reprinted with kind permission from The Huffington Post UK. Please visit www.huffingtonpost.co.uk for further information.

University clearing: a view for and against

***An article from* The Conversation.**

By Elizabeth Houghton, PhD candidate in Sociology, Lancaster University and Bhavik Patel, Reader in School of Pharmacy and Biomolecular Sciences, University of Brighton

A-level results day sees highs and lows for many thousands of students across the country waiting to receive their grades. For every jubilant smile relieved to have secured a place at university, there is also the anxious grimace of the student who hasn't quite made the grade.

Last year, 41,530 students went into clearing – the process universities use to fill spaces they have left on courses with those who didn't make it into their first choice – meaning roughly 10% of all students found their way to university this way. But does the system actually work?

Below, two experts give their thoughts on the highs and lows of the clearing system:

The current system needs reforming

Elizabeth Houghton is a PhD candidate at Lancaster University, whose research looks at how 'marketised' higher education can impact student choice.

The advice around clearing is consistently framed as 'don't panic'

– but with increasing evidence of the difference in job prospects and salaries of graduates from different ranks of universities – it is easy to understand why a sudden change could come as a shock to the system.

The reality of the university admissions system is that students must sell themselves to universities, but universities also need to sell themselves to students. And while clearing phone lines are often presented as 'helplines', they are also in reality sales lines.

The onus is on applicants to scramble for places in a 'highly competitive environment' when universities actually need students – and the revenue they bring. Especially now the cap on student numbers is off. For some universities clearing is one way to bump up intake and income.

Instead of the current system, we need to develop an effective admissions policy that gives students the chance to apply to university with the most important information: their grades. This reformed system would follow the logic of clearing, and give students the chance to apply for university after they have received their grades – taking some of the panic out of the process.

But it is clear we are still some way off that point, given the way clearing currently operates. This raises some timely questions for anyone serious about the need for student choice in higher education – whether it operates in market terms of not.

Clearing is a major asset to students

Bhavik Patel is a biochemist at the University of Brighton, who came through clearing to study at the university.

"I know better than most about the clearing process and have seen first hand how the experience has changed dramatically over the years. When I went through clearing ten years ago, it was nerve-racking and you didn't know how to approach universities.

"Back then, it was often shrouded in a dogma of failure. For universities, being in clearing was seen as a sign of weakness, that they were unable to fill course spaces. But now, clearing is a major asset to students.

"So as clearing comes around again this year, students should be seeing it as an opportunity, not a setback.

"It provided me with a second chance in life and made me more focused. It made me determined to prove I was better than the grades. This determination led to be winning the GlaxoSmithKline Emerging Scientist of the Year Award. And in 2015 I won the Royal Pharmaceutical Society's Science Award, which is presented to a scientist with a proven record of independent research and published work that shows outstanding promise – not bad for someone who didn't make the grades.

"My career has seen me travel to different countries working with some of the top names in science. Without clearing, none of this would have happened. It has truly helped to shape me into the scientist I am now."

From being a process where students would be judged, clearing is now the norm and has become a vibrant process of opportunity, where students may even obtain places on courses at universities they seldom felt they could achieve.

19 August 2016

Student choice: the new proposals are all froth and no coffee

The Government claims it will offer students a wide-ranging menu of university options. But diversity won't just happen by itself – it needs planning.

By Gordon Meckenzie, Chief Executive of GuildHE

This Government says it is a great champion of student choice. Yet it is on the brink of legal reforms that risk restricting the options to the kind of choice car-maker Henry Ford famously offered customers in the 1920s: "a car painted any colour that he wants so long as it's black".

The diversity of UK higher education is one of its outstanding strengths. Large multi-faculty universities in big cities, smaller specialist universities for subjects like agriculture, performing arts and creative art and design; musical conservatoires; institutions founded by the churches; higher education in FE colleges; new providers opening up new areas of specialism, such as modern music. Students aren't homogenous; institutions should not be either.

But the Government isn't doing enough to preserve and promote the different types of university that are essential to real choice. When some members of the House of Lords have tried to help them do more by amending the Higher Education and Research Bill, they have been stonewalled.

Fix the Funding

The Government says it wants to encourage flexible learning and see more people completing full degrees in just two years. But so far it hasn't taken the opportunity provided by its own bill to remove the obvious barrier and fix the funding. Some of the newer, private providers have tried to innovate – but they face an uphill struggle.

So why not look at setting a total cost limit for a degree rather than an annual fee? Or, if you really want greater innovation and flexibility, look at funding by academic credit.

Widening the range of higher education providers isn't just good for students. It's good for the economy too. Universities that specialise have close links to the professions, industries and creative sectors they serve. Teachers and researchers are often industry professionals. They help students understand the world they want to work in and help businesses use research to innovate.

It's as if the bill hasn't caught up yet with the Government's industrial strategy. That strategy says "place" matters, and that every part of the country needs to reap the benefits that universities can bring: better skills, a more productive workforce, and research that helps companies turn ideas into new products and services and sell them round the world.

Creative-focused universities alone contribute at least £8.4 billion to the UK economy. But these benefits they bring cannot be taken for granted. They depend on central decisions about funding and regulation as much as on choices by students.

That is why the Lords have been right to try to improve the bill, including by encouraging government to report any need for new providers; for example, where there are skills shortages, not enough part-time provision, or places that are lagging behind because they don't have a university.

As Baroness Wolf said, when introducing the amendment: "Diversity will not happen by magic."

Leaving it to the market

The Government's response is that is has already done enough because the new Office for Students (OfS) will have duties to promote choice and encourage competition.

But leaving it to the market won't work. And what if the OfS interprets its job narrowly, as being about choice of courses? Then the decisions about money and how you regulate and what you plan won't happen in ways that support and encourage truly diverse learning environments.

The OfS should have a clear duty to promote and maintain diversity. The newly announced preferred candidate for its chair, Sir Michael Barber, might even agree. He once co-authored an essay on higher education called *An Avalanche is Coming*, which said that if you didn't want to be swept away you needed to understand there would be no single successful model of a university. "On the contrary," it argued, "diversity will be the key."

The Government is fond of fast food analogies when it comes to higher education – often repeating references to McDonald's and Byron Burger – so here's one for the risk they're running: a sector where student choice looks increasingly like most high streets – plenty of places to buy a cappuccino, so long as you don't mind sitting in a Costa or a Starbucks.

8 February 2017

⇨ The above information is reprinted with kind permission from *The Guardian*. Please visit www.theguardian.com for further information.

300,000 more university places needed to keep up with demand for degrees, study says

"It is difficult to see how the policy of uncapped student recruitment can continue under the current finance model".

By Eleanor Busby, Education Correspondent

Hundreds of thousands more university places will be needed by 2030 to keep up with a growing demand, a new study has predicted.

A cap on student numbers may need to be introduced if demand continues to rise and more pressure is placed on funding, the report from the Higher Education Policy Institute (HEPI) think tank said.

At least 300,000 more places will be needed at English universities due to a boom in the number of young people and a continuing rise in students going into higher education, the research suggested.

Between 2010 and 2016 there was a 5.5 per cent increase in undergraduate numbers despite a decline in the number of 18-year-olds, the study said.

This decline in the population is due to halt next year, and over the next decade, as the 18-year-old population in England is set to rise by nearly 23 per cent.

If this was the only factor, demand for degree courses would rise by around 50,000 places by 2030, the study says. But the participation rate – the numbers of young people aged 20 and under going into higher education – has increased by nearly 25 per cent since 2006.

The study calculated that if participation also increases over the next 12 years at the same rate as the average of the last 15 years, then 350,000 more full-time places will be needed by 2030.

It said that the main factor that could have a negative impact on demand is Brexit, which could mean that numbers reduce by around 56,000.

The report concluded that the most likely outcome is that by 2030, a net increase of around 300,000 full-time places will be needed.

"This analysis has serious implications for higher education policy," the report warned, adding: "Present arrangements imply an open-ended government cheque book since recruitment is unconstrained, and each student recruited is entitled to a loan that is subsidised (and, since the Prime Minister's intervention in October 2017 more heavily subsidised) by taxpayers."

It said: "A driver of the review of post-18 education that has recently been established is concern over the high cost to graduates of loan repayments. It is difficult to see how that will be addressed without additional government expenditure.

"Some form of control over student numbers is likely to be required, especially if the subsidy for those who do participate in higher education is to be maintained, let alone increased."

Bahram Bekhradnia, HEPI president, said: "Given the fact that each new student recruited (with few exceptions) represents increased demand for government-subsidised student loans, it is difficult to see – under the current finance model – how the policy of uncapped student recruitment can continue.

"This is particularly pertinent given the constraints on public expenditure and the absence of any suggestion from the Treasury that more money will be available for higher education in the future."

Under the current system, home and EU students going to English universities pay up to £9,250 a year in tuition fees, and can get government loans to cover the cost.

15 March 2018

⇨ The above information is reprinted with kind permission from *The Independent*. Please visit www.independent.co.uk for further information.

Tuition fees and access to higher education

In 2012, the Government raised the maximum cost of university tuition fees from £3,000 to £9,000 a year, and that has since risen to £9,250. How has that affected the number of people going to university, and has it put off those from disadvantaged backgrounds?

UCAS is one of the main providers of higher education statistics, and it measures disadvantage in a number of ways. This ranges from looking at where a school pupil lives (POLAR3), to also considering their sex, ethnicity and school-type (MEM), and whether or not they get free school meals (FSM). We focus mainly on those three metrics, looking at rates of entry to UK universities and other higher education institutions among pupils in England.

Record numbers of 18-year-olds are entering higher education, across all different advantage levels in the last decade. The difference in entry rates between those from the most advantaged backgrounds, and those from the most disadvantaged backgrounds had been falling. However, in the last few years this trend has stalled somewhat, and in the last two years the gap has begun to rise again on some metrics. This rising gap began a few years after the introduction of £9,000 fees, but we can't say if they are linked, or what would have happened had fees not been raised.

A lot of the metrics show a dip in entry rates among 18-year-olds from all advantage groups in 2012 (the year £9,000 fees were introduced) – but this dip only tends to last a year. Entry levels were extremely high in 2011 (most likely to avoid higher fees), making levels in 2012 comparatively low. By 2013, entry levels generally began increasing again.

The number of 18-year-olds entering higher education has risen in every year since 2012, whilst the number of people aged 20 and over has dropped off since 2015.

Throughout this piece we're talking mainly about entry rates to higher education. That's the percentage of

people accepted into higher education in a given year. The majority of higher education institutions are universities, but it also includes colleges – where you can study for qualifications including a work-related diploma or a higher level apprenticeship.

Students from the most disadvantaged areas

One way UCAS measures disadvantage is by looking at an 18-year-old's likelihood of entering higher education based upon where they live. Called POLAR3, the measure divides small areas of the country into five groups, from those in most disadvantaged areas to most advantaged.

Across all POLAR3 groups, higher education entry rates have increased since 2012.

A higher level of 18-year-olds from the most disadvantaged areas are in higher education than ever before – 20% of that group entered higher education in 2017, compared to 15% in 2012, and 11% in 2006.

Pupils from the most disadvantaged areas are still less likely to enter higher education, but the gap in entry rates has been narrowing since 2006 (as far back as the data goes). Progress has slowed in the last couple of years, however.

In 2006, those living in the most disadvantaged areas were around four times less likely to enter higher education than those from the least disadvantaged areas. That figure was around three times in 2012, and in 2017 it was around twice as likely.

A wider measure of disadvantage

The Multiple Equality Measure (MEM) looks at educational disadvantage using a wider range of background characteristics, again sorting pupils into five groups.

In 2017, 18-year-olds from the most advantaged group were around four times more likely to go into higher education than those in the least advantaged group.

The gap had been narrowing consistently since 2006. However, this has stopped in the last two years.

This measure is more experimental and is missing some students, as UCAS has to match higher education entrants in their data with school pupils in the National Pupil Database. It's not always possible to do that, and in such cases pupils are not counted in the MEM data.

Free school meals pupils

When looking at students who were in receipt of free school meals (FSM) at

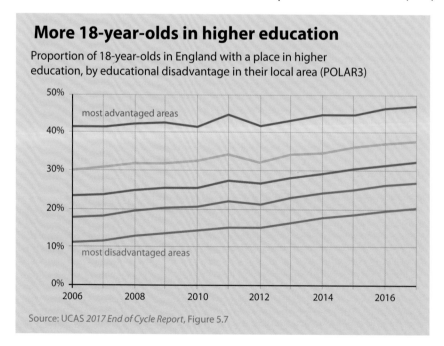

More 18-year-olds in higher education

Proportion of 18-year-olds in England with a place in higher education, by educational disadvantage in their local area (POLAR3)

Source: UCAS *2017 End of Cycle Report*, Figure 5.7

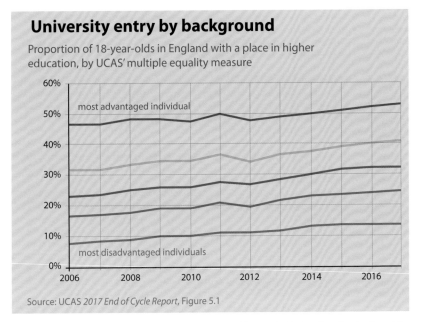

University entry by background

Proportion of 18-year-olds in England with a place in higher education, by UCAS' multiple equality measure

most advantaged individual

most disadvantaged individuals

Source: UCAS *2017 End of Cycle Report*, Figure 5.1

the age of 15, we see a similar trend in how the gap in entry levels had been falling over time, before rising again slightly in the last couple of years.

In 2017, 17% of 18-year-olds who received FSM went into HE, compared to 34% of non-FSM pupils. So non-FSM pupils were twice as likely to enter higher education as those receiving FSM.

There had been a general narrowing of the gap since 2006 (the earliest data we have), when pupils not receiving FSM were around three times more likely to enter higher education. This has stopped in the past two years.

The Government publishes its own separate data on FSM pupils in England going into higher education.

Unlike UCAS, it also includes 19-year-olds in its data.

Compared to UCAS' data, the government figures find entry rates to be higher among all FSM groups, and the difference between the most and least disadvantaged slightly narrower. Among 18- and 19-year-olds starting higher education in 2014/15, 24% of those who received a FSM at age 15 entered further education. Non-FSM pupils were roughly twice as likely to go into higher education than FSM pupils. That's slightly lower than UCAS' figure for that year.

The UCAS data shows the gap between the two groups increasing from 2015 onwards. Government data is not yet available for those years – so we don't know if they also found this trend.

Access to the most selective universities

Some universities are more competitive to get into, and the gap in entry rates is greater in these cases.

UCAS divides higher education providers into three groups based on the average grades among accepted applicants. Higher tariff providers are more selective as they require the highest grades, and UCAS told us the vast majority of higher and medium tariff providers are universities or medical schools.

2.5% of 18-year-olds from the most disadvantaged MEM group went to a higher tariff provider in 2017, compared to 14% from the most disadvantaged group going to any higher education institution.

The gap in entry levels between the most and least disadvantaged groups is also wider when looking at higher tariff providers. Those from the most advantaged group were around ten times more likely to go to a higher tariff university in 2017 than those from the most disadvantaged group. For entry to any higher education institution, the gap is four times.

That gap in entry rates between the most and least disadvantaged has been falling consistently over time though.

These trends are very similar when using the POLAR3 metric instead of MEM.

Access by age

18-year-olds-make up 52% of all people who entered higher education in 2017. Since 2015, the number of higher education entrants has levelled off or declined for all age groups – except for 18-year-olds, whose numbers have continued to increase. In the first year of £9,000 fees, the number of 19-year-olds entering higher education dropped significantly.

Drop-out rates

Once disadvantaged students are in higher education, they are more likely than their peers to drop out.

8.8% of young students from the most disadvantaged POLAR3 group left higher education after their first

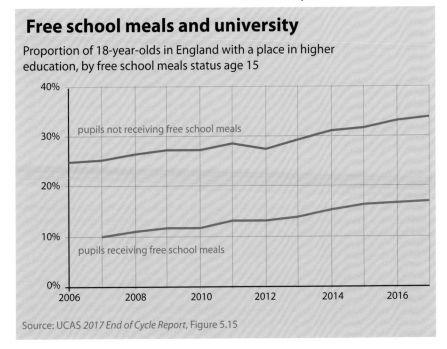

Free school meals and university

Proportion of 18-year-olds in England with a place in higher education, by free school meals status age 15

pupils not receiving free school meals

pupils receiving free school meals

Source: UCAS *2017 End of Cycle Report*, Figure 5.15

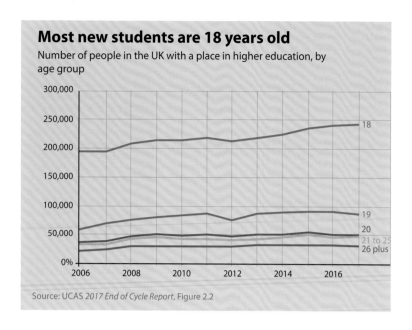

Most new students are 18 years old

Number of people in the UK with a place in higher education, by age group

Source: UCAS *2017 End of Cycle Report*, Figure 2.2

year in 2014/15. That's the highest level since 2009/10, when it was 9.3%. In comparison, the drop-out rate for students from the fifth most advantaged areas stayed relatively stable at 4.9%.

15 March 2018

⇨ The above information is reprinted with kind permission from *The Independent*. Please visit www.independent.co.uk for further information.

More than 40,000 fewer part-time students go to university due to tuition fees hike, study suggests

"The Government needs to reverse the catastrophic decline in part-time students."

By Eleanor Busby, Education Correspondent

More than 40,000 fewer part-time students are going to university because of the hike in tuition fees in England, a new study suggests.

The Government's introduction of higher tuition fees exacerbated the decline of part-time students in England, preventing many "second chance routes" to social mobility, the report from the Sutton Trust charity states.

There were more than 40,000 fewer part-time students in 2015 than five years before – when tuition fees had not yet risen to £9,250 a year for full-time undergraduates, it reveals.

If entrant numbers for those living in England had fallen by the same proportion as those living in Wales – who did not experience tuition fee increases – then there would have been 149,000 part-time students in England in 2015, instead of 106,000, it adds.

The number of part-time students in England declined by 51 per cent

between 2010 and 2015 – and researchers say part of the fall was caused by higher tuition fees in 2012.

The drop in part-time and mature study is preventing those who may not have followed the traditional route from school – or whose work or family responsibilities make full-time study impractical – from going into higher education, the report warns.

The proportion of young people in part-time study from disadvantaged backgrounds is almost 50 per cent higher than for full-time courses.

It has been published just weeks after the Government announced its long-awaited review of university funding.

Theresa May admitted that allowing universities to charge variable tuition fees had left Britain with "one of the most expensive systems" in the world.

Sutton Trust has called for the costs of part-time tuition to be tackled to stop the dramatic decline.

Students who are eligible for the new part-time maintenance loan should be able to take out a tuition fee grant for the first two years of their course, the report recommends.

Sir Peter Lampl, founder of the social mobility charity said: "Part-time study is a crucial second chance for many people. This report shows that it has been decimated. The major reason for this dramatic decline is the introduction of big increases in tuition fees. Mature and part-time students have a better understanding of the consequences of taking on debt than young full-time undergraduates.

"The Review of Post-18 Education should acknowledge there is no 'one size fits all' approach to student finance, and recognise that the mature and part-time sector requires tailored solutions.

"Opportunities to get on in life should not be restricted to a one-off decision at age 18. Genuine social mobility would empower all those in society to gain the skills they need to succeed, regardless of age or background. Part-time and mature education is key to this."

Peter Horrocks, vice-chancellor of the Open University, said: "The 2012 funding changes provoked a crisis in part-time higher education in England, hitting students from disadvantaged backgrounds particularly hard.

"Businesses are crying out for skilled workers, yet the best way of training people – by allowing them to learn while they earn – is being undermined. The UK Government has the chance to reverse the catastrophic decline in the number of part-time students in its forthcoming review of funding."

Universities UK recently launched a project, with the Confederation of British Industry (CBI), looking at the fall in part-time students over recent years.

Professor Julie Lydon, vice-chancellor of the University of South Wales and chair of the project's advisory group, said: "If the UK is to prosper and compete internationally, this must be looked

at by policy-makers. It is important, therefore, that it is addressed in the Government's forthcoming review of higher education in England."

University group Million Plus said that the Government's review of tuition fees in England should make the recruitment of mature and part-time students a priority.

A Department for Education spokesperson said: "Everyone who wants to access higher education should be able to. We know that studying part-time and later in life brings enormous benefits for individuals, the economy and employers and we want this to continue.

"We already offer loans for all types of students, including those who are part-time, but we recognise the difficulties faced by some students, which is why for the first time ever we plan to introduce full-time equivalent maintenance loans in 2018/19 to

support those people who want to study part time.

"The Prime Minister also made clear last month that we are undertaking a major review of post-18 education and funding to ensure that the system is giving everyone a genuine choice between high-quality technical, vocational and academic routes, and students and taxpayers are getting value for money. This includes more flexible routes, like part-time study."

15 March 2018

⇨ The above information is reprinted with kind permission from *The Independent*. Please visit www.independent.co.uk for further information.

© independent.co.uk 2018

Target of three million apprenticeships and new funding system risk poor value for money

By Neil Amin-Smith, Jonathan Cribb and Luke Sibieta

In April 2017, the Government is introducing an 'apprenticeship levy' (a 0.5% tax on an employer's paybill above £3 million per year), which is estimated to raise £2.8 billion in 2019–20. At the same time, it is introducing more generous subsidies for employers training apprentices in England. However, government spending on apprenticeships in England is only expected to increase by £640 million between 2016–17 and 2019–20. So most of the revenue raised is being spent elsewhere.

This new funding system is intended to help the Government meet its commitment that there will be three million apprenticeships starting in England between 2015 and 2020. However, the significant expansion and design of the new system risks it being poor value for money. Specific

elements of the system could end up being particularly damaging to the public sector.

It is already the case that 44% of new apprentices are aged 25 and over and the new target is likely to increase this fraction. There is a risk that the apprentice 'brand' is becoming just another term for training.

These are among the conclusions from new analysis of reforms to apprenticeship funding by IFS researchers, which forms part of the forthcoming IFS Green Budget 2017, produced in association with ICAEW and funded by the Nuffield Foundation. The analysis examines the new system for funding apprenticeships and its potential effects. It finds that:

Although the apprenticeship levy increases taxes on large employers,

the new subsidies for employers to train apprentices mean that employers will have to pay nothing, or at most 10%, of off-the-job training costs for apprentices, up to certain price caps set by the Government. This will increase the incentive to employers to hire apprentices, particularly those aged 19 and over for whom employers paid at least 50% of training costs prior to 2017.

This zero or near zero cost of training poses considerable risks to the efficient use of public money. Employers will have little incentive to choose training providers who can provide training at a lower price. Employers will also have a big incentive to re-label existing training schemes as apprenticeships.

The target of an average of 600,000 new apprentices a year in this parliament is a 20% increase on the level in 2014–15. This large expansion risks increasing quantity at the expense of quality. Although the Government is trying to increase the quality of apprenticeships, the Institute for Apprenticeships may come under pressure to approve new apprenticeships quickly. Ofsted will take on an expanded (and welcome) role with respect to inspecting training providers and employers. However, it has already expressed serious concerns about the quality of apprenticeship schemes, particularly those created more recently.

The apprenticeship levy will put downward pressure on wages. The Office for Budget Responsibility assesses that it will reduce wages by about 0.3% by 2020–21. While only 2% of employers will pay the levy, at least 60% of employees work for employers who will pay the levy.

The Government has set every public sector employer with at least 250 employees in England a target that 2.3% of their workforce must start an apprenticeship each year. This takes no account of big differences between organisations. Unless existing employees start apprenticeships, the targets imply around one-in-five new public sector hires must be an

apprentice. Such a blanket policy cannot be an efficient way to improve skills in the public sector. It risks costly reorganisation of training and inefficient ways of working. These targets should be removed.

The Government has also failed to make a convincing case for such a large and rapid expansion in apprenticeships. In seeking to justify these changes, it quotes statistics that show a collapse in employees' training. However, better measures of training show a much more modest decline. The Government also makes wildly optimistic claims about the extra economic activity or earnings such investment in apprenticeships could generate (with quoted benefit-to-cost ratios of over 20:1). While there is a clear need for a better-trained workforce, this cavalier use of statistics risks undermining what might be a perfectly sensible case for a gradual expansion of apprenticeships in areas where quality can be assured.

Neil Amin-Smith, an author of the report, said: "We desperately need an effective system for supporting training of young people in the UK. But the new apprenticeship levy, and associated targets, risk repeating

the mistakes of recent decades by encouraging employers and training providers to relabel current activity and seek subsidy rather than seek the best training. There is a risk that the focus on targets will distort policy and lead to the inefficient use of public money."

Jonathan Cribb, another author of the report, said: "With the subsidies for apprentices' training costs at 90% or 100%, employers are encouraged to take on more apprentices. But this also provides them with little or no incentive to choose a training provider with a lower price. In addition, the specific targets for most public sector employers in England to employ apprentices could lead to costly, and potentially damaging, re-organisations, and should be dropped."

31 January 2017

⇨ The above information is reprinted with kind permission from the Institute of Fiscal Studies. Please visit www.ifs.org.uk for further information.

UCAS warns surge in unconditional university offers means students may take "foot off the gas"

Exclusive: The head of the admissions service says the sector must have an "open and honest" debate about the issue.

By Eleanor Busby, Education Correspondent

Education bosses have called for an urgent rethink on universities offering 'unconditional offers' to students following a massive surge in the number of places being given out regardless of final exam grades.

Clare Marchant, head of the universities and colleges admissions service (UCAS), said the sector needed to have an "open and honest" debate

about the issue after figures showed a 40 per cent rise in unconditional offers received by school-leavers last year was a "concern".

Last year, more than 50,000 students were offered unconditional places, raising fears universities were using the practice to secure student fees of more than £9,000 a year, to the detriment of some pupils.

"I think the sector having an open and honest discussion about the impact of unconditional [offers] is really important," Ms Marchant told *The Independent*. "[Some universities] are using it in an across-the-board way and that is probably of the greatest concern."

Her comments come after concerns were raised by Robert Halfon, chair of the Education Select Committee, who

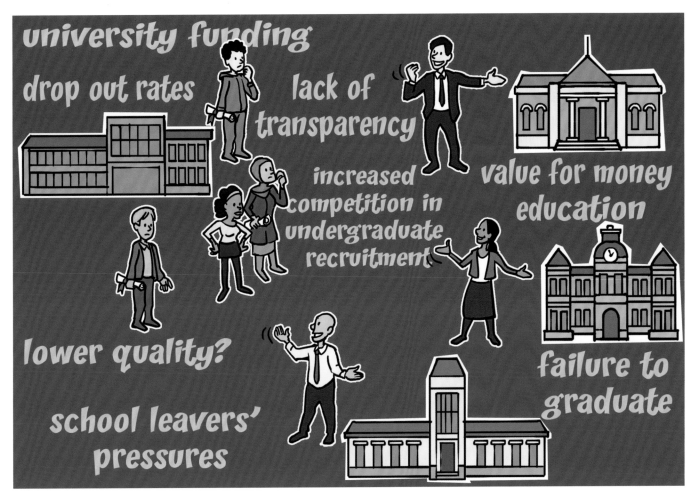

said he was "hugely concerned" by the issue.

Last night, he urged universities minister Sam Gymiah to look again at the trend, which he accused of "dumbing down" standards.

Mr Gymiah warned last week that a growth in unconditional offers could undermine the "excellence" of universities across the country.

The minister said institutions should not make unconditional offers as a way of "sidestepping" the key criteria used when selecting whether people will succeed at university.

Unconditional offers are not limited to vocational subjects at less prestigious universities. Computer science and biological sciences are among the subjects with the highest proportions of unconditional offers being given out, a recent report from the universities admissions service shows.

Ms Marchant warned students not to forget the importance of A-level grades and urged them not to rush into accepting unconditional offers that might not be right.

She said: "Our advice to students is two-fold. First, keep your foot on the gas because those A-levels and other qualifications stay with you for life.

"You will have them on your CV when you are 40-plus and applying for a job.

"Second, don't make the choice on the back of an unconditional. Think about what choice you would have made anyway."

The number of unconditional offers received by 18-year-olds from England, Northern Ireland and Wales rose by 40 per cent in a year – from 36,825 in 2016 to 51,615 in 2017, UCAS's annual report revealed in December last year.

The rapid rise of unconditional offers has come as universities compete to fill uncapped places on £9,250-a-year courses. "It is a buyer's market and students are in the driving seat and therefore with no limit on numbers,

universities want them and this is one way to get them," Ms Marchant said.

School-leavers with predicted A-level grades of BBB or ABB were more likely to receive an unconditional offer than those predicted AAA this year, the latest UCAS report found.

Ms Marchant, who was appointed as chief executive of UCAS last year, said she'd "keep an eye" on the trend of unconditional offers being offered at lower predicted grades than before.

4 March 2018

⇨ The above information is reprinted with kind permission from *The Independent*. Please visit www. independent.co.uk for further information.

Five tips for starting university

By Eloise Lavell

For some of you, knowing which part of the country you will be starting a new life in has you bubbling over with excitement for the upcoming adventures: Freshers' week, moving out of your parents' house for the first time and making new friends. Others, however, will find the prospect of being left alone in an unfamiliar place, with unfamiliar people absolutely terrifying. If you are filled with anxiety about what the next academic year holds in store for you, don't worry – we are here to help! Here are five tips to help set yourself up for a happy university life.

1. Knock on doors!

If you have moved into halls of residence, don't sit in your room and wait for a social life to come to you – just go knocking! Remember, everybody is new, alone and looking for friends. Try your own flat first, and get to know the people you will be spending the next year with, but also remember to knock on other flats in your building – introduce yourself, maybe ask what their plans are for the evening. They will most likely be grateful to you for including them, as they will be finding this experience slightly daunting as well!

If you can, try and make plans for the next day during this time. Your first morning waking up alone in your new bedroom, is usually when it all sinks in – you are here to stay. If you have something to get up and out for, you are more likely to feel positive about this realisation rather than scared or homesick (which are still completely normal feelings at this point).

2. Get involved

The prospect of joining a society or club can seem a little scary, but there really is no better time to do it, than at the start of term when everyone else is new and scared as well! Most universities have a 'Freshers' Fair' where all the societies set up stalls to encourage people to join. You might already have a hobby to get involved with, but if not, just go along and find at least one thing you're interested in joining. Maybe your new flatmates or someone from your building will want to go with you too.

3. Explore your new city

One of the most exciting and nerve-racking things about going to university, is the unfamiliarity of your surroundings. So go and explore, with or without your new acquaintances, and find your local convenience store, pharmacy or pub. The more you discover about your new city and what it has to offer, the quicker you can settle in and feel at home!

4. Admit when you're feeling homesick

Nobody likes to admit they're having a tough time or missing home, especially on social media, but I guarantee you the majority are feeling it. During your first term everyone seems to be under the misconception that you must appear to be having fun with a large group of people at all times of the day and night, and if you aren't constantly out with a posse of ten-plus more people, then you have no life. This is not true! Just like when you lived at home, it is still perfectly normal to want some downtime, or to skip the club and watch a film instead. You are likely to have homesick days when you feel a little lonely or are craving those lovely home comforts; if and when these days occur, tell someone about it! Whether it's an old friend from home or a new friend at university, you might be surprised to find out that they have been experiencing similar apprehensions – it's very unlikely you're alone in feeling like this.

Also, remember that there will be support and counselling available at the university, should you feel uncomfortable, or unable to talk to any peers about this, or any other problem you may be facing.

5. Have fun

This is the most important tip of all – surround yourself with positivity and good friends and the fun will be sure to follow. If I could give one crucial piece of advice to people about to start university, it would be to never waste your time with people who bring any negative energy into your life – you don't owe them anything. A few close friends is way more beneficial to your happiness and mental health than holding onto tons of half-friends or acquaintances if they're just grinding you down. This is your time, you are in control, so enjoy it!

13 September 2016

⇨ The above information is reprinted with kind permission from Ditch the Label. Please visit www.ditchthelabel.org for further information.

Student budgeting: how to create a student budget

Our quick and easy guide on creating a student budget. Discover how to create your own personal student budget in just six simple steps.

Knowing how to make the most of your money is important for a great student experience at university. With this in mind, we've put together a six-step guide to help you to take control of your new financial situation and get a first in managing your finances.

Evaluating your expenses might not be at the top of your to-do list, but invest some time in your financial future now and you'll profit from it later. And it's easier than it sounds! Grab your calculator and follow our six steps below to create your very own student budget.

How to create a student budget in six easy steps

1. Work out your income for the term

Pull out your student finance letters and work out how much money you have available for the term. This should include your student loan, any bursaries or scholarships, and all other income you will be receiving during the term.

2. Consider the necessities

Calculate how much you need to spend on essential costs that you can't avoid, such as accommodation fees and bills, and deduct this from your available money. Make sure to put this aside and don't spend it before it's needed.

3. Split it into weekly chunks

Once all your essential costs have been accounted for, you should have a clearer idea of how much you have left to spend on other living costs. Divide your remaining amount by how many weeks there are in the term to get a weekly allowance.

4. Estimate your weekly living costs

Work out how much you will need to spend on living costs each week, for example on food, and deduct this from your weekly allowance. Try not to forget the little extras such as laundry, toiletries, gym memberships, TV subscriptions and travel costs.

5. Don't forget to factor in the fun stuff

Living on a student budget doesn't mean you can't have fun – in fact the more you stick to your budget, the more fun you can afford! With the remaining amount, give yourself a weekly spending limit for social activities such as nights out and the occasional takeaway.

6. Be conscious of where your money is going

Get in the habit of writing down your spending (even if it's just on a note on your phone) to help you to stay on track. Use online banking to check your bank balance often and keep tabs on how much you are spending to make sure you don't overspend. Review your budget regularly and don't be afraid to change it if it's not working for you.

Getting a part-time job

If you find yourself wanting a little bit more in your pocket then you might want to consider getting a part-time job alongside your studies.

Guildford is bursting with shops, cafés and restaurants, all within walking distance of the University, and there are lots of opportunities to find work and earn some extra spending money at Surrey. We also have our very own student recruitment agency on campus, Unitemps, who can support you in finding your perfect part-time job.

26 July 2017

⇨ The above information is reprinted with kind permission from the University of Surrey. Please visit www.surrey.ac.uk for further information.

© 2018 University of Surrey

Top Tip:

Open a second bank account (remember you could be eligible for a student account) and put your student loan in there each term, then pay yourself a monthly salary to keep a constant trickle of money coming into your account.
This puts a hard limit on your spending and means you have something to fall back on should you need to. And finally, don't forget to keep some money aside to allow you some flexibility when you need it.

You now have all of the information you need to manage your money effectively at university!
Living on a student budget will teach you organisation and planning skills that will be useful throughout your life.

Prime Minister's announcement on changes to student funding

This House of Commons briefing paper discusses the announcement of changes to the student finance system by the Prime Minister on 1 October 2017. It gives an overview of past changes to the student finance system, outlines current debate and analyses the potential impact of the proposed changes.

On 19 February 2018, the Prime Minister announced that there would be a 'wide-ranging review into post-18 education' led by Philip Augar. The review is to look at how future students will contribute to the cost of their studies, including 'the level, terms and duration of their contribution.' The Prime Minister discounted the idea of moving back to a fully taxpayer funded system. It is expected that the review will report in early 2019.

This paper will be updated with any relevant information or changes that come from the review process.

The student finance system has gone through a prolonged period of change and reform since the Labour Government introduced upfront university tuition fees of £1,000 per year in 1998.

Since 1998, tuition fees have progressively risen. In 2006, under the Labour Government, the Higher Education Act 2004 trebled fees to £3,000 per year and introduced deferred variable fees and tuition fee loans which are repaid after graduation.

From 2006, fees rose gradually by inflation until 2012 when, under the Coalition Government, tuition fees were raised to £9,000 per year following an independent review of the student finance system by Lord Browne. The student finance reforms at this time also included raising the repayment threshold to £21,000 and introducing a variable tiered rate of interest on student loans.

Most changes in the student finance system have been made in response to a particular set of funding pressures. The cumulative effect is that England now has the highest 'public' tuition fees in the industrialised world and a complicated system of student support.

Since 2012 there have been further changes which have moved student support increasingly away from non-repayable grants and towards loans. Maintenance grants and NHS bursaries have been abolished and replaced by increased loans, the student loan repayment threshold has been frozen and interest rates on student loans have increased.

In addition to these reforms, a process called the Teaching and Excellence Framework has allowed higher education institutions with high-quality teaching to raise their fees by an inflationary amount to £9,250 in 2017/18 – this is the first fee rise since 2012.

The combined effect of these changes has been to increase student debt – the Institute for Fiscal Studies has calculated that students from the poorest backgrounds will accrue debts of £57,000 from a three-year degree.

In the 2017 General Election, the Labour Party manifesto included a commitment to abolish tuition fees and to restore maintenance grants. This proposal proved popular among young voters.

On 1 October 2017 the Prime Minister announced that there would be changes to the student finance system:

⇨ the fee cap would be frozen at £9,250

⇨ the repayment threshold would rise to £25,000

⇨ there would be a review of the student finance system.

The proposed freeze on fees will reduce income for universities, compared to what they expected to receive. It will also mean that the Government will need to lend, and students to borrow, slightly less.

Increasing the threshold to £25,000 reduces future repayments and hence increases the economic costs, or subsidy element of the loans. The proportion of borrowers with some debt written off could increase from around 70% to around 80%. The annual cost could be in the order of £2 to £3 billion.

6 March 2018

⇨ The above information is reprinted with kind permission from parliament.uk. Please visit www. researchbriefings.parliament.uk for further information.

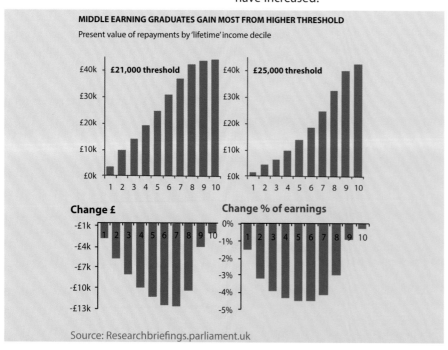

MIDDLE EARNING GRADUATES GAIN MOST FROM HIGHER THRESHOLD
Present value of repayments by 'lifetime' income decile

Source: Researchbriefings.parliament.uk

Scholarships, grants and bursaries – extra funding for your degree

By Karen Kennard

Karen Kennard, director of social enterprise The Scholarship Hub, which helps students find additional funding for their university studies, tells us about the different ways you can get extra funding towards your degree.

Recent years have seen a huge increase in the number of scholarships being offered to students and despite popular belief you do not have to be an academic genius who has grown up in poverty to be eligible. Equally, even if you did not apply or qualify for any entry scholarships, you should not stop looking while you study. There is funding out there open to first, second, third and fourth year students and postgraduates as well as prospective students.

But you have to look for it.

What is the difference between a scholarship, grant or bursary?

Scholarships are usually given as rewards for achievements, grants for things you want to do but can't afford to do and bursaries as a bonus when you are struggling financially, but this is not a hard and fast rule and the terms are often used interchangeably. However, the basic principle of each is the same – this is money that is awarded to you which you do not have to pay back.

This money can be awarded for many different reasons depending on the type of organisation that is awarding it. Different organisations will have different motives.

If you understand the different types of funding that is available it will be easier for you to identify where you might fit the eligibility criteria, but bear in mind there are also some scholarships which are open to all students.

What are the different reasons scholarships, grants and bursaries are given?

Academic Excellence: offered to students who achieve specified grades and they are not always the top grades as you might expect. It is worth bearing in mind that Academic Scholarships are not just offered by the universities themselves, but quite often professional associations or institutes offer scholarships to encourage a new generation of talent in their industry.

Musical Scholarships: if you are a talented musician or singer and would be happy to perform while at the university you could get a music scholarship. You do not have to be studying music.

Personal Circumstances: Scholarships that are based on things that are specific to your personal circumstances, such as where you live, if you've been in care, what your parents do or your religion. These might come from local authorities, religious organisations or charities.

Financial Need: More traditional type of scholarships, award money to individuals who are in financial need. These are more often called grants or bursaries and can be offered either by the university or charities and trusts.

Sporting Achievement: If you have made outstanding achievements in sport, many universities offer scholarships to attract the best talent. You will have to compete for the university in your sport.

Company Scholarships: More and more companies are starting to offer scholarships and some include work experience as part of the offer. These are increasingly being offered to raise awareness of a particular company among their future customers and so will target students studying specific subjects. Sadly, some universities are less willing to share these types of scholarships with their students and so awareness of these is low but the plus side is that this can increase your chances significantly of winning one if you know about it.

Your interests and hobbies – there are some scholarships which are based on your extra-curricular activities such as showing a commitment to social engagement or improving the lives of others.

Other scholarships – increasingly there are more scholarships being offered by companies, where all students have to do is submit an essay or video – in reality they are just student competitions but the money has to be used for your tuition fees. Currently many of these are coming from America, (and the money awarded is US Dollars) where scholarships are big business and they are now opening these up to UK students. Make sure you read the terms and conditions of these scholarships as they will quite possibly be looking for some PR or be using the applicants' contact details for further marketing but again, as long as you are aware of this, you could win large amounts of money.

Where can I find this additional funding?

All students should keep an eye on their own university website for funding opportunities. New ones are being added all the time and they are not just for prospective students, so make a regular visit to the relevant pages to check what's available.

However, many universities will only promote scholarships which are specific to their particular university and there are many opportunities which are open to students at any university. The Scholarship Hub is a comprehensive database of all scholarship opportunities open to UK/EU students. It allows you to search for scholarships based on subject, university or for the more generic scholarships.

There are also thousands of smaller charities and trusts which offer educational grants. You can find information on these in the *Guide* to *Educational Grants*, which can be found in most reference libraries.

20 March 2017

⇨ The above information is reprinted with kind permission from the National Union of Students. Please visit www.nus.org.uk for further information.

Is the tide turning on tuition fees?

By George Nixon and Tom Mitchell

Ever since Tony Blair's government introduced tuition fees 19 years ago, the idea that a university education should cost something has been a staple of government policy. Which is why it makes it all the more interesting when the first secretary of state Damian Green, one of the PM's closest confidants, and the Deputy Prime Minister in all but name, says we should have a "national debate" on tuition fees.

Aides to Mr Green, and the Universities Minister Jo Johnson, were quick to point out that this was not a suggestion of a rethink on government policy, but merely that it should explain that it's either tuition fees or higher taxes. But over the last few weeks, culminating in Shadow Education Secretary Angela Rayner being granted an emergency debate in Parliament on the subject, the tide seems to be turning towards the possible abolition of tuition fees. And with the Lady who is for U-turning the embattled resident of Number 10, could this follow the 'dementia tax', the public sector pay cap, and possibly Brexit itself into the out tray?

It's worth reminding ourselves how it is we got to this position that would have seemed unthinkable even a year ago. First, the undeniable success of Jeremy Corbyn's wooing of the student vote in 2017 put the issue of student debt and university fees front and centre in the election that was supposed to be about Brexit. I've been on record that it's patronising rubbish to suggest that the policy of abolishing fees was the sole reason why Labour attracted young voters in huge numbers, but there's no doubting that being greeted on your 21st birthday with £50,000 worth of student debt is a big issue to many people my age. And perhaps a massive student turnout that helped evict the Ashford MP's neighbour Sir Julian Brazier from his nearby Canterbury seat made him realise that the Tory Party is losing a demographic battle.

Then came a landmark report from the respected think tank the IFS two weeks ago, which found that most will now finish university with an average debt of £50,000, which 77 per cent of graduates will never pay off. This prompted an interesting piece from former Number 10 Policy Unit chief Lord Adonis, the architect of the £3,000 'top-up' fees introduced by Labour in 2004. His argument can essentially be summed up by this quote: "How did we get from the idea of a reasonable contribution to the cost of university tuition, to today's Frankenstein's monster of £50,000-plus debts for graduates on modest salaries who can't remotely afford to pay back these sums while starting families?"

The problem therefore with these spiralling fees, which seem set to be raised even further, is twofold. Firstly of course the level of debt that graduating students are burdened with, which is also supplemented by interest rates of up to 6.1%. The fact that previous Chancellor George Osborne was able to, in effect, retrospectively change the terms and conditions on those tuition fee loans by upping their interest rates to a variable rate above inflation after students had already taken them out is entirely reprehensible.

Furthermore, that level of debt, and the fact that according to the IFS two-thirds will never pay that back, creates something of a black hole in the Government finances, seeing as that money that is paid out via the Student Loans Company is never coming back. Intriguingly, Adonis raised the point that the intention was that, while capped at £3,000, fees "would vary between £1,000 and £3,000, depending on the cost and benefit of the individual course". In practice of course, we know what happened. Fees were set across the board at the maximum £3,000, which then became £9,000 under the Coalition Government.

The counter-argument, of sorts, was raised by personal financial guru Martin Lewis on 5 Live. The point was that, while yes you are going to graduate with a lot of debt, if you are going to have a system whereby university education does cost, the current system we have is probably the best you can aim for, in terms of the fact you have to earn £21,000 before you start paying anything back, and how it is wiped after 30 years.

Therefore, this means that this is less a personal finance-based argument and more an ideological one. And if the last few weeks are any indication, we seem to be headed for a collision course between those who believe in tuition fees, and an increasing number who want them abolished. Whether that leads to a system that Adonis originally envisioned, where degrees are priced according to their relative merits, their resource use and hours of teaching, or they are abolished all together, it seems that since 8 June the tide does appear to be turning against tuition fees.

22 Jul 2017

⇨ The above information is reprinted with kind permission from Backbench. Please visit www.bbench.co.uk for further information.

Night owl students perform worse academically due to 'social jet lag', study finds

Students who go to bed later should avoid earlier classes, experts suggest.

By Sabrina Barr

It is often said that when you go to university, you're only able to achieve two out of these three fundamental student necessities: having enough sleep, maintaining a social life and obtaining good grades.

Lack of sleep can take its toll on your grades, especially if you're a 'night owl' by nature following an 'early bird' schedule.

A recent study has discovered that students who typically go to bed late and wake up early for class suffer academically when they fail to take their circadian rhythm into account.

They wind up experiencing self-imposed 'social jet lag', which can result in a drop in grades.

In the study published in *Scientific Reports*, the researchers assessed the activity of 14,894 students enrolled at Northeastern Illinois University as they logged onto the establishment's learning management system over the course of four semesters, from autumn 2014 to spring 2016.

The researchers were able to document whether students could be categorised as 'larks', 'finches' or 'owls' by noting when the students scheduled their classes and tracking their activity levels on the days that they didn't have class.

Aaron Schirmer, associate professor of biology at Northeastern Illinois University, and Benjamin Smarr, a postdoctoral fellow at the University of California, discovered that as many as 50 per cent of the students had chosen to attend classes that took place before they were fully alert.

Ten per cent of the students had already reached their peak level of alertness before attending class.

For the 40 per cent who opted to attend classes in sync with their body clocks, they consequently performed better academically.

"We found that the majority of students were being jet-lagged by their class times, which correlated very strongly with decreased academic performance," said Smarr.

"Different people really do have biologically diverse timing, so there isn't a one-time-fits-all solution for education," he explained.

Schirmer and Smarr believe that rather than encourage students who naturally go to bed later to try to hit the hay earlier, they should attempt to fit their class schedule around their circadian rhythm in order to reap the benefits.

"Rather than admonish late students to go to bed earlier, in conflict with their biological rhythms, we should work to individualise education so that learning and classes are structured to take advantage of knowing what time of day a given student will be most capable of learning," Smarr said.

"It's really important for students to think about the timing of their activities to try to optimise their educational efforts," said Schirmer.

3 April 2018

⇨ The above information is reprinted with kind permission from *The Independent*. Please visit www.independent.co.uk for further information.

Five key learnings and habits from a 2:1 graduate

By Celine Henry, History and Politics Graduate, University of Hull

My university experience was an amazing journey with un-ending development and growth. Hopefully, these five key lessons/habits from what was an amazing experience will inspire someone.

1. Speak with your lecturers

Studying two disciplines was quite fulfilling, however the tricky part was the fact that both departments required different styles of essay formatting and methods of assessments. Half-way through my first year I began arranging meetings with my lecturers and I saw a massive improvement in my work as I took their advice and tips on board, especially on essay formatting as writing essays were a strong point. I am quite happy that I had the opportunity to do this earlier on in first year as by my final year I could explore different modes of writing as well as speak to a variety of academics just for help whether they were my supervisor or not.

Caution: sometimes you may ask questions based on your or your lecturer's interest that will incur a ten minute answer. In the event of such a predicament make sure you have eaten prior to the meeting and timed the conversation in order to catch your bus back home!

2. Make friends with your course mates and build your adult network

Often my house mates would laugh at how I was never at home during the day. Whilst it was severe I can say that my times spent with course mates were absolute blessings. I cannot count how many times I realised I had learnt a theory or date wrong leading up to an exam, to which these were all resolved by course mates. Additionally, hanging out with my course mates boosted my confidence to make contributions in seminars and lectures. Essentially, everyone is often shy but when we do become comfortable with each other that will propel great conversation and fulfilling learning. By doing this I realised that I was not in competition with any of my course mates but rather they had rather become a part of my 'network'. To have a dynamic reach of people from all over the United Kingdom and the world who were striving to make some kind of impact wherever they would find themselves was deeply inspiring and I saw this as a privilege.

3. Pray (or meditate)

I developed a habit of praying and journaling as regularly as I could; this helped massively when there was no one around. University can be a very lonely place despite the many support systems that may be available. I loved these moments because it helped me to also understand myself more. I finally understood what graduates meant by "uni is a place you learn about yourself". It was I alone reflecting on my character and deeply thinking and planning my visions for the future as I was inspired. Praying helped me to calm down during the time I would worry about the future. You may not be deeply religious or necessarily have a faith, however I found these times crucially important and helpful than anything I attempted to enhance myself whilst at university.

4. Have a life inside and also outside of university

As a student, you are most likely not able to engage with the locals effectively besides when you popped into the local Lidl (the supermarket every student should make their best-friend!). I made the conscious decision to engage with the locals a little more by my second year which was also an amazing experience. I was fortunate enough to be part of a church community, volunteered at museums along with many other activities which taught me a lot and fuelled a sense of independence in me. This independence boosted my confidence to attend talks and events on interesting topics as well as travel alone, which was my ultimate highlight.

5. Identify your educational weaknesses and make efforts to face them

I mentioned that writing essays were a strong point for me. On the other hand was my nemesis: exams. If I could ever meet the man who created this phenomenon I would do anything to beg him to rethink such a traumatising experience. I do not usually suffer from anxiety attacks or any of that sort, however throughout education taking exams had always been an uncomfortable experience. It was not until my final year that I realised that I needed to identify it as an academic weakness and seek help. It was a tough time for me, having to attend exam skills classes and revising whilst maintaining a level of calmness and belief in myself. However, I can say it was truly liberating knowing that after facing this weakness, there was candid help available.

Essentially, you are there for a certain amount of years that you will never get back. For some this may be your last hurdle with education – and that is why identifying your shortcomings with your learning is crucial in reaping the best you can. You are paying £9k+ after all! Make your educational investment worth it and you won't regret it.

10 August 2017

⇨ The above information is reprinted with kind permission from Elevation Networks. Please visit www.elevationnetworks.org for further information.

Coping with exam stress

Exam season is the most stressful time of year for many students.

Sarah Gillborn, Vice President Welfare at Leeds Beckett Students' Union, tells us about 'Stress Less Fest' and how students can stay on top of things.

Why did Leeds Beckett SU begin running 'Stress Less Fest'?

We started running Stress Less Fest simply because we know that the weeks leading up to the exam period can be a really stressful time. We want to encourage students to take time out for themselves and to look after themselves during this period, and rather than putting out a leaflet or some form of publication with ways to destress, we thought the best way to do it is to bring the de-stressing activities to the students!

What have been your most successful activities, and how effective have they been in helping students?

In previous years we have had a puppy room, where students can come and play with young guide dogs for a small donation. This is really great as not only do people get to play with adorable puppies, but it also means the dogs get to be socialised with people, so it's win-win! We also give out free fruit, and this always tends to go really quickly.

But I think the most effective thing we do is just being really visible to students. Just by being there to give out fruit, and asking them how they've been getting on, a lot of students take the opportunity to let off some steam, and we can remind them of how proud they should be of their hard work, and that we are always here if they need any further support.

How important is it that students take their mental health and well-being seriously?

Mental health and well-being is really important to students, and to everyone. Whether we are well or not, we all have mental health, and we are all at risk of becoming unwell if we don't look after ourselves or if we don't feel that we have adequate support in place. It's really important that students look after themselves, aren't afraid to ask for help when it is needed, and take time out for themselves when they feel like they are being snowed under.

What advice would you have for students who feel they are struggling with exam stress?

If you are struggling with exam stress, first and foremost you should talk to someone. Whether it's family, a friend, a course mate, or a trusted teacher or lecturer. Talking about it with someone will help you to figure out why you're feeling stressed, whether it's workload or if there's something you can't get your head around, and

people who you trust can help you to overcome any overwhelming stress you might feel. Also, again, it is really important to take time for yourself. Start revision early, so that you can spread it out more, and make sure that you have plenty of time to rest and to relax with friends.

Who can students contact for support?

Students can always come to their students' union for support. Whether it's your welfare officer or students' union advice team, or even just a friendly member of staff, there will always be someone here who can support you themselves or direct you to someone who will be able to help. You also shouldn't underestimate the support you can get from your friends. Stress is not an unusual thing to feel, especially during assessment periods, and although it affects us all in different ways, we can all share our stress-busting tips, and things are much easier to deal with when you're not dealing with it alone!

March 2016

⇨ The above information is reprinted with kind permission from the National Union of Students. Please visit www.nus.org.uk for further information.

© 2018 National Union of Students

More students choosing to live at home and commute

More than 328,000 students in the UK elected to remain in their family home last year. With tuition fees rising and living costs at their peak, is the traditional 'student lifestyle' becoming a privilege only the wealthy can enjoy?

By Amanda Cashmore

Part of the attraction of going away to university used to be just that – moving away from home and gaining long-awaited independence. But something has changed in recent years; more and more students are choosing to sacrifice that freedom in favour of saving a buck.

Recent HESA figures show more than 328,000 students in the UK elected to remain in the family home last year. But with living costs on the rise and monthly rent in London now at a whopping average cost of £1,508 per month, it hardly comes as a surprise. The age of the student waster is dead: the Millennial generation is one of soft drink consumers and long-suffering commuters.

Alice, 22, lives in Kent and pays £477 per month for her daily four-hour commute to and from Islington. She says she really struggles with missing out on aspects of student life: "Most of my friends are lucky enough to live in London but unfortunately I just can't afford it. It's such a shame because when they want to go to the pub after uni I usually have to say no because I have to tutor and drive home from the station.

"It's upsetting because in my undergraduate degree I had barely any contact time so didn't make many friends on my course, whereas on my MA I have loads of contact time and friends, but I'm missing out because I can't socialise with them."

The constant travelling is incredibly draining, as she has a part-time tutoring job outside of her studies – meaning she is rarely home before 10pm, reheating her dinner and climbing into bed before it all starts again at 6am. "I feel I can't dedicate myself to my studies as much because

there is literally no time," Alice adds. "I cannot afford to live in London, but I cannot magic more hours to make it worth my while."

In order to cut commuting time, some students choose to stay with significant others who do live in the city rather than spend multiple hours a day travelling. Amelia, 23, lives near Milton Keynes and says she will only go home during the week when she has to, as the time she loses on her daily three-hour commute takes too much of a toll. Her boyfriend, Youssef, lives in halls right in the centre of London.

She explains that her staying over most week nights has caused the couple to become more serious: "If I lived in London we might not spend as much time with each other, because it would mean we could go to and from each other's flats – it means I'm either at home or with him, and because my course is so intense it means we're together more often. For example, last year we lived in opposite ends of Norwich and we'd see each other three times a week, now it's most weekdays."

Amelia adds that the commute, besides being expensive, impacts her studies. The stress of turning up late and flustered to lectures following train delays leaves her feeling stressed and unprepared for the day.

Of course, there is the issue of maintaining a social life alongside studying. Although the idea of missing nights at the pub after lectures does not sound like anything to lose sleep over, it is important for those who are completing an intensive course to have a strong support network.

Mimi, 21, completed her undergraduate degree at UCL while living with friends, but chose to move back in with her father in an outer London suburb

whilst achieving her master's degree at City University. She finds the aspect of going out with friends a "massive hassle" as staying out past midnight means she needs to find a place to stay, and it takes all the spontaneity out of a night out with friends when you do not have a spare toothbrush: "It's always a bit icky staying at someone else's house when you don't have all your things with you."

Despite the many drawbacks of being a commuter, certain students claim they would prefer it to their halls of residence. Sarah, 22, lives in halls of residence and pays an extortionate £950 per month for an ensuite room with a shared kitchen. She says the cost of living in the capital is not worth it at all for her, and she would commute from her home in the Midlands if it were possible: "Now I'd rather be fed for free." The postgraduate student does admit that the halls are in prime location, a mere ten-minute walk from her university campus, but she thinks the necessity for living so close is more necessary for first-year students, who require more independence when first starting university.

Another student said that her arduous commute was a contributing factor to her decision to defer her studies for a year. Meg, 21, found her commute from Bat & Ball in Kent isolating, explaining: "I didn't realise how much it would affect me – it had a lot more of an impact than I thought it would."

Meg quickly found herself overwhelmed with how exhausted she became, and began drinking copious amounts of coffee to stay awake in lectures – which did not help her anxiety problems. She acknowledges that the constant delays on her train line made her feel less and less inclined to go to lectures; once you know you'll be two hours late, it makes it difficult to make the trek for only another two hours of more university.

Meg found her consistent tardiness challenging, and out of character: "I've never been someone that's late, but because of the trains I became that person."

Alongside the commuting is of course the transition back to living with parents. No matter how close a 20-something may be to their family, learning to live in a family unit after three years of independent living at university is never easy. Meg says the commute itself brought out a snappy, irritable side in her that does not usually appear: "I get on really well with my family, but I was so tired and stressed that I would lash out when

they would ask me questions, which is obviously not what I want to be doing."

How to cope if you're a student commuter

University College London's Welfare Officer, Mehj Ahmed, is a student commuter herself and recognises that the constant travelling is exhausting. She recommends several tips for postgraduates who are feeling the strain:

⇨ Plan your meals

⇨ Eat well before morning commutes, the long days mean students will require more energy

⇨ Use your commuting time

⇨ Get your work done – failing that, download a mindfulness app to relax in a busy carriage.

⇨ Join commuter Facebook groups

⇨ Find people going in the same direction as you. Mehj explains that it helps to know that 'we're all in the same boat of expensive travel and endless journeys'.

1 February 2017

⇨ The above information is reprinted with kind permission from *The Independent*. Please visit www.independent.co.uk for further information.

More young people are going to university

"More young people are going to university than ever before, including more young people from disadvantaged backgrounds."

Claim

Record numbers of young people are going to university, including more people from disadvantaged backgrounds.

More 18-year-olds are going to university than ever before, as are young people from disadvantaged backgrounds. Participation by disadvantaged young people has levelled off slightly by some measures in the past year, but the longer term picture is generally one of increasing numbers.

Advantaged students are still substantially more likely to go to university than their disadvantaged peers.

This piece looks specifically at the numbers of young people going to university, rather than those applying. We've covered that in more detail here. In summary, the number of 18-year-olds applying to university across the UK was at a record high in 2017. The application rate in England was also at a record high, though it fell in Wales and Northern Ireland. The proportion of people from disadvantaged

backgrounds across the UK applying to university is also at a record high, though these figures only go up to January 2017.

Record rate of young people accepted to university in England and Wales

There were 238,900 18-year-olds in the UK accepted onto a full-time university course in 2016, the most ever recorded. This made up around half of all acceptances via UCAS that year.

Around 33% of all 18-year-olds in England were accepted into a university place in 2016 – the highest level recorded. In Wales it was around 30%, again the highest on record.

Entry rates for 18-year-olds in Northern Ireland rose to 35% in the year to 2016, the same level as 2014.

We haven't mentioned Scotland here because not all universities in Scotland use UCAS and data issues have affected the comparability of Scottish figures over time.

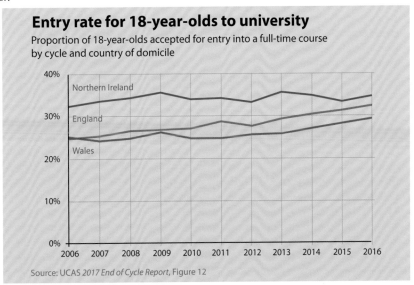

Entry rate for 18-year-olds to university

Proportion of 18-year-olds accepted for entry into a full-time course by cycle and country of domicile

Source: UCAS *2017 End of Cycle Report*, Figure 12

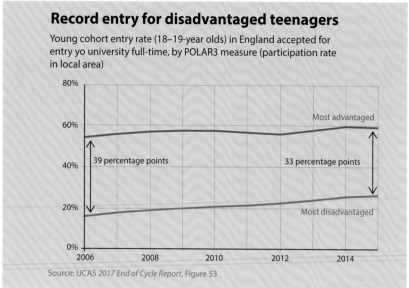

Record entry for disadvantaged teenagers

Young cohort entry rate (18–19-year-olds) in England accepted for entry yo university full-time, by POLAR3 measure (participation rate in local area)

Most advantaged

39 percentage points

33 percentage points

Most disadvantaged

Source: UCAS *2017 End of Cycle Report*, Figure 53

In Northern Ireland it was at 16%, the second highest recorded level.

Disadvantage here is measured according to the rate of participation in higher education by young people in each area, so the most disadvantaged areas are those with the lowest rates of participation by young people.

The rate for those in the most advantaged areas in 2016 increased slightly to 46% in England, Northern Ireland and Wales.

The cohort entry rates (available only for England), show the gap between young people from the most disadvantaged areas and the most advantaged areas going to university is decreasing.

UCAS have also released a new 'multiple equality measure' (MEM), for the first time for 2016.

This looks at things like gender, ethnic group, where a person lives, the type of school they go to, and if they got free school meals. Based on a combination of these factors 18-year-olds are placed into one of five groups ranging from most to least disadvantaged.

On this measure all five groups have seen growing participation rates, and reached record highs in 2016. That said, the participation rate for the most disadvantaged group has increased more slowly than that of the other groups over the last two years.

Disadvantage can also be measured by income level, typically measured by whether or not a young person was receiving free school meals at age 15.

The entry rate to university of 18-year-old state school pupils in receipt of free school meals was also at a record high in 2016 – at about 16%. That's compared to almost 33% for those who didn't receive free school meals.

The equivalent government measure (which looks at entry to university by age 19) showed a slightly different picture when Ms Greening made her comments. By this measure there was a slight fall in the proportion of pupils receiving free school meals who had gone to university by 2013/14. It decreased by one percentage point to 22%. This decrease was also seen among those not receiving free school

Of course, some people wait until they're 19 before starting university. There's another set of data that includes these people alongside the 18-year-olds who started the year before – what's called the cohort entry rate. This was also the highest on record in England and Wales in the group entering age 18 in 2015 and age 19 in 2016.

This all comes from UCAS data. Separate figures from the Government show a similar picture. The Government provides data on how many students are living in England who have been in higher education (for the first time) for at least six months and are aged 17–20. This data has the benefit of including part-timers, while the UCAS data relates only to full-time applicants. But it takes a bit longer to get published, so it's two years behind the UCAS data.

The participation rate for this age group was an estimated 41% in 2014/15 (the latest year available), almost the same as it was in 2011/12 when it was the highest on record. The government statisticians say that particularly high participation in 2011/12 "appears to have been predominantly driven by more students choosing not to defer entry in that year in order to avoid having to pay a higher tuition fe".

Using the same measure the participation rate for 18-year-olds in 2014/15 was 26%, the highest on record and just above what it was in 2011/12.

And the same is true for disadvantaged young people

In 2016, the entry rate for 18-year-olds living in the most disadvantaged areas increased for all countries in the UK. It increased to the highest on record in England (almost 20%) and Wales (18%).

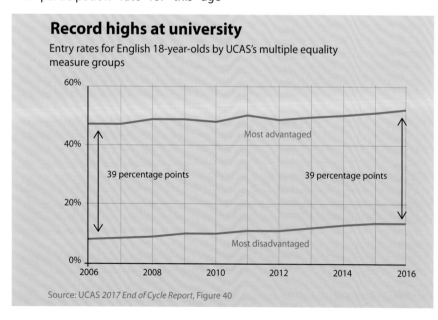

Record highs at university

Entry rates for English 18-year-olds by UCAS's multiple equality measure groups

Most advantaged

39 percentage points

39 percentage points

Most disadvantaged

Source: UCAS *2017 End of Cycle Report*, Figure 40

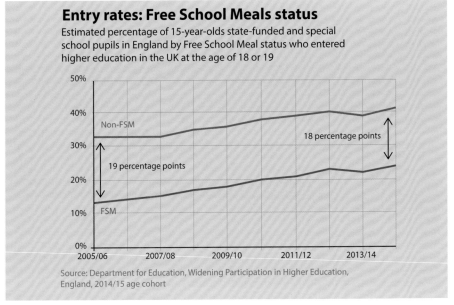

Entry rates: Free School Meals status

Estimated percentage of 15-year-olds state-funded and special school pupils in England by Free School Meal status who entered higher education in the UK at the age of 18 or 19

Non-FSM

18 percentage points

19 percentage points

FSM

50%
40%
30%
20%
10%
0%

2005/06   2007/08   2009/10   2011/12   2013/14

Source: Department for Education, Widening Participation in Higher Education, England, 2014/15 age cohort

is increasing. It was 24% for those attending university by 2014/15.

Conclusion

Mostly correct at the time, and now correct on all measures. Some figures produced by government statisticians showed a slight dip in the proportion of disadvantaged students attending university when the claim was made. Newer data now suggests that this was temporary and that the longer term picture is one of generally increasing numbers.

Updated 22 September 2017

⇨   The above information is reprinted with kind permission from Full Fact. Please visit www.fullfact.org for further information.

© 2018 Full Fact

meals, so it didn't change the gap between the two.

The Government told us that it can't say whether or not the introduction of higher tuition fees had an impact on the dip in entry rates for students receiving free school meals who attended university by 2013/14 – the first cohort of 18- and 19-year-olds to be affected.

Newer figures have become available since which show that this seems to have been a temporary effect and that overall the proportion of people who received free school meals and attend university by the age of 19

How has the student population changed?

Over the next few weeks students will be travelling to university for the start of the academic year. Understanding student populations and the impact they have on an area is complicated by many factors, but what can ONS data tell you about students in the UK?

Student numbers have almost doubled since 1992.

Young people aged 18 to 24 in full-time education, seasonally adjusted, UK, March to May 1992 to May to July 2016

In the period March to May 1992, there were 984,000 people aged 18 to 24 in full-time education. In May to July 2016, there were 1.87 million, approximately one in every three people, aged 18 to 24 in full-time education.

Looking at the employment rate amongst this group you can clearly see students gaining employment during the holidays. Students in 2016 are less likely to be in employment than 20 years ago, with on average 35.4%

having a job in June to August 2015 to May to July 2016 compared with 40.3% in the same period 20 years previously. However, those that do have a job are more likely to keep it throughout the entire academic year, this is reflected by the fact that the peaks and troughs in the data are less pronounced in 2016 than they were two decades ago.

Inward and outward migration is likely to be greater around larger universities

Many of the local authorities that contain leading Russell Group universities, have a peak of people moving into the area at age 19 – when students tend to start their studies. Typically there is also a smaller but similar peak of people moving out of the area at age 22 when students typically finish university.

Looking at the percentage of in and out migration by local authority you can see common patterns in those that have a major university compared with those without.

Average annual projected migration in and outflows (internal, cross-border and international moves), England, 2014 to 2024

Internal migration of students and graduates is likely to influence the economic structure of an area; young people in rural areas may move away from their local authority to gain a university education elsewhere. However, once their student life comes to an end they may choose not to return, perhaps due to a lack of career prospects or forming a relationship with someone who lives elsewhere. This may cause a reduced skills base in some local authorities without universities. In London there are many universities and there is perceived to be a much larger and more varied graduate labour market, this may contribute to inward migration at ages 18 to 22.

As well as the changes in overall population, a large student population within a local authority may influence

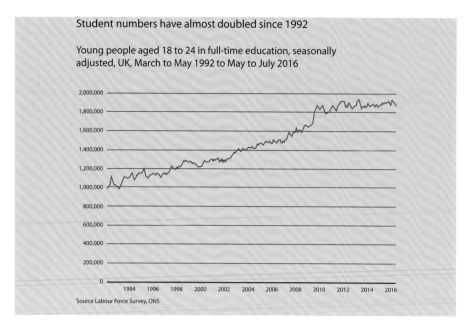

Student numbers have almost doubled since 1992

Young people aged 18 to 24 in full-time education, seasonally adjusted, UK, March to May 1992 to May to July 2016

Source Labour Force Survey, ONS

the overall birth rate in that area, as students in higher education tend to have a below average birth rate.

Average annual projected migration in and outflows (internal, cross-border and international moves, England, 2014 to 2024)

Local authorities that neighbour those with Russell Group universities are likely to show similar but opposite peaks in migration. People aged 19 move out of the area whilst people move into the area aged 22. This is likely to be due to students moving away to university and returning three years later.

It's important to highlight that these projected migration figures are also influenced by international, cross-border and non-student internal migration. London areas in particular are affected in these ways.

The aged 18 to 24 population in Oxford and Cambridge increases by over 80% during university term-time.

Age profile of the usually resident and out of term population: Oxford, 2011

The population of an area can vary at different times throughout the year, placing different requirements on the provision of services locally. In Oxford in 2011, there was a 12% increase in the overall population and an 83% increase in the 18- to 24-year-old population during term-time compared with out of term-time.

The male to female ratio can change in areas with universities during term-time.

In 2011, during university term-time in Runnymede there were 87 men aged 16 to 24 for every 100 women in the same age group. Out-of-term time, the number of men in this age group increases to 99 per 100 women. This may be because Royal Holloway College (part of London University) is in Runnymede. It has a strong reputation for Arts and Humanities subjects which have traditionally attracted more female students.

Stafford, and Charnwood in Leicestershire, also experience fluctuations in sex ratios aged 16 to 24, with 18 and 13 fewer men per 100 women respectively out-of-term time than in term-time. The presence of Staffordshire and Loughborough Universities nearby could be a factor as both have a reputation for courses that may attract a greater number of male students.

International student numbers have fallen and are at their lowest since 2007

Over a quarter of immigrants come to the UK for formal study. In 1977, there were 29,000 international students, rising to a peak of over eight times this amount in 2010. However, recent years have seen a decline in long-term immigrants arriving to study, with numbers falling to 164,000 in the year ending March 2016.

20 September 2016

⇨ The above information is reprinted with kind permission from the Office for National Statistics. Please visit www.ons.gov.uk for further information.

© Crown copyright 2018

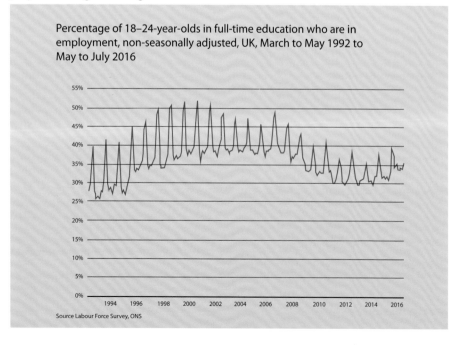

Percentage of 18–24-year-olds in full-time education who are in employment, non-seasonally adjusted, UK, March to May 1992 to May to July 2016

Source Labour Force Survey, ONS

Social mobility and universities

By Claire Milne

Claim

More people from deprived backgrounds are going to university than ever before.

It's correct that private school pupils are still disproportionately represented in top professions and among University of Oxford undergraduates.

It's also the case that there are more 18-year-olds from disadvantaged areas going to university than ever before in England, Wales and Scotland, according to UCAS figures. In Northern Ireland it is the second highest on record. On this measure, the gap between disadvantaged pupils and advantaged pupils across the UK has narrowed in the last ten years, although it is unchanged in the last year.

> **"There are more people from deprived backgrounds going into universities than ever before."**
>
> **Bernard Jenkin MP,
> 7 December 2017**

A disproportionate number of private school pupils go to Oxford

Around 44% of young, undergraduate full-time students attending the University of Oxford in 2015/16 went to an independent school, according to the latest data from the Higher Education Statistics Agency.

Looking at the third most selective universities in England, around 23% of state school pupils who took A-levels or equivalent qualifications went to these in 2014/15, compared to 65% of pupils at independent schools.

This gap is the largest it has been since 2008/09 (as far back as these figures go). The gap is smaller looking just at pupils who took A-levels.

Across the whole of England, 7% of students were attending an independent school in January 2017.

That's the same proportion as it's been since at least 2003.

An analysis of 'leading people' in the UK by the social mobility think tank The Sutton Trust found that private school pupils were disproportionately represented at the top of many of the UK's professions.

It found that in 2015 around three-fifths of top doctors went to private school, almost three-quarters of top military officers and top judges and around a third of UK-educated FTSE 100 CEOs. Around half of the senior civil service and top journalists were privately educated.

Looking at the latest intake of MPs following the June 2017 election. The Sutton Trust also found that 29% were privately educated.

The proportion of disadvantaged young students going to university is increasing

In 2016, the proportion of 18-year-olds living in the most disadvantaged areas going to university increased for all countries in the UK. It increased to the highest on record in England (almost 20%), Wales (18%) and Scotland (11%). In Northern Ireland it was at 16%, the second highest recorded level.

> **"When you look at the top of almost all the major professions and look at universities like Oxford, that are taking in more kids from state school, but I think it's still around 40% from private school and only 7% of the population go to private school, I think social class remains as big an issue in the UK as it's ever been"**
>
> **Richard Bacon,
> 7 December 2017**

Compared to 2006, the gap between the proportions of disadvantaged and advantaged students going to university has narrowed across all four countries. In the past year, the gap has stayed broadly the same.

Scotland's figures shouldn't be directly compared to those from the rest of the UK because there is a substantial chunk of higher education provision in Scotland not included in these figures.

Disadvantage here is measured according to the rate of participation in higher education by young people in each area of the country, so the most disadvantaged areas are those with the lowest rates of participation by young people. There are a number of other ways to measure disadvantage and we've looked into them in more detail here.

Looking at pupils in England receiving free school meals, an increasing proportion are going to university by age 19, according to figures from the Department for Education. An estimated 24% of English pupils receiving free school meals had gone to university by the time they were 19 in 2014/15 – the highest on record.

The gap between students not receiving free school meals and those who do has remained at around 17–18 percentage points over the last eight years, based on these figures.

Conclusion

In 2016 the proportion of 18-year-olds living in the most disadvantaged areas going to university was the highest on record for England, Scotland and Wales. It's the second highest level it has ever been in Northern Ireland.

8 December 2017

⇨ The above information is reprinted with kind permission from Full Fact. Please visit www.fullfact.org for further information.

© 2018 Full Fact

Are more working-class students dropping out of university?

"Many working class and part time and older mature students are actually leaving university... there's record levels of students that are actually having to leave university before they finish their qualifications, and I think that's because of the Government's policies."

By Claire Milne

Claim

Record levels of working class students are leaving university before completing their degree.

The proportion of young students from disadvantaged areas leaving higher education in England after their first year is at its highest level in five years, but isn't the highest ever recorded.

Across the UK, and in England where the UK Government controls education policy, the proportion of students dropping out a year into their first full-time degree increased slightly over the last two years. Over time it has remained steady or generally decreased depending on which type of students you look at.

Overall, mature students are more likely to drop out of full-time degrees than younger students, although the proportion doing so has been decreasing. Mature students are less likely to drop out of part-time degrees than younger students.

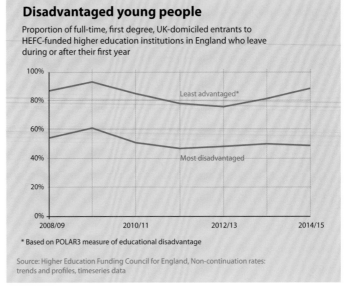

Disadvantaged young people

Proportion of full-time, first degree, UK-domiciled entrants to HEFC-funded higher education institutions in England who leave during or after their first year

Least advantaged*

Most disadvantaged

* Based on POLAR3 measure of educational disadvantage

Source: Higher Education Funding Council for England, Non-continuation rates: trends and profiles, timeseries data

HESA told us that it doesn't publish any data on why students are choosing to continue or not with their courses.

Students from disadvantaged areas leaving higher education after a year are at their highest level in five years

Aside from students from the most advantaged areas, the proportion of UK students leaving higher education in England before their second year of study has increased over the last two years according to the Higher Education Funding Council for England (HEFCE). Ms Rayner's office pointed us towards a report by the Office for Fair Access which used these HEFCE figures.

8.8% of young students from the most disadvantaged fifth of areas undertaking their first full-time course left higher education after their first year in 2014/15. That's the highest level since 2009/10, when it was 9.3%. So it's a bit lower than the highest level recorded.

In comparison, the drop-out rate for students from the fifth most advantaged areas stayed relatively stable at 4.9%.

The gap between students from the most and least advantaged areas has also widened since 2012/13.

Students who drop out in later years aren't measured in these statistics, which we'll discuss later on.

Disadvantage here is measured according to the rate of participation in higher education by young people in each area, so the most disadvantaged areas are those with the lowest rates of participation by young people.

This measure doesn't look specifically at individuals' socio-economic backgrounds. HEFCE says that "POLAR classification measures a specific form of disadvantage, namely educational disadvantage, in the form of a young person's likelihood of progressing into HE based upon where they live.

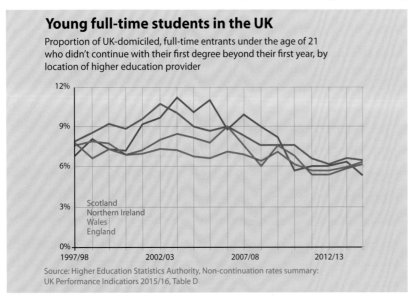

Young full-time students in the UK

Proportion of UK-domiciled, full-time entrants under the age of 21 who didn't continue with their first degree beyond their first year, by location of higher education provider

Scotland
Northern Ireland
Wales
England

Source: Higher Education Statistics Authority, Non-continuation rates summary: UK Performance Indicatiors 2015/16, Table D

Estimating educational disadvantage is not usually the primary purpose of other measures of disadvantage, and although there is known to be a correlation between disadvantage in general and a young person's chances of progressing into HE, the correlation is not always strong."

As well as the figures above, Ms Rayner's office pointed us to a separate report which looked at the link between the proportion of students at a university whose parents had 'lower-level' jobs and the rate at which that university's students didn't complete their degree, and found that students from lower socio-economic backgrounds were more likely to drop out.

This report didn't look at trends over time.

Research from the Institute for Fiscal Studies also found that those in higher socio-economic groups were more likely to complete a degree than those in lower socio-economic groups.

The proportion of students leaving higher education in the UK is generally decreasing or stable

"Non-continuation rates among young, full-time first degree students

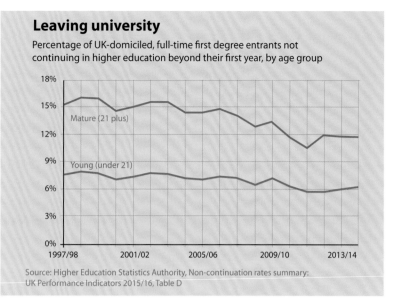

Leaving university

Percentage of UK-domiciled, full-time first degree entrants not continuing in higher education beyond their first year, by age group

Source: Higher Education Statistics Authority, Non-continuation rates summary: UK Performance Indicators 2015/16, Table D

[in the UK] has remained relatively steady over time with a more downward trajectory observed for mature entrants", according to the Higher Education Statistics Authority (HESA) which publishes the figures.

The proportion of students under the age of 21 not continuing in higher education in the UK in their second year of study was 6.2% in 2014/15.

It was highest for students at universities in Scotland (6.5%) and lowest in Northern Ireland (5.3%).

New mature students are more likely to drop out of full-time degrees, but fewer have been

Ms Rayner also mentioned mature students in her interview.

The proportion of mature students (those over the age of 21) not continuing with higher education after the first year of their full-time degree is generally higher than for those under the age of 21. It was 11.7% across the UK in 2014/15.

Across the UK the proportion of mature students not continuing beyond

the first year of their first degree has changed most considerably in Northern Ireland. 2011/12 saw the lowest drop-out rate in Northern Ireland at 7.3%, but it has since returned to 15% in 2014/15 – the highest on record, and closer to the levels seen in 1997/98.

Overall, the individual countries of the UK have seen the drop-out rate among mature students generally decreasing since 1997/98, though they have levelled off or increased in the last few years.

Looking at students starting university again (as in, those not first-time entrants), younger students are slightly more likely to drop out. Both proportions have generally been declining over the last 20 years.

The proportion of young part-time students who aren't continuing with higher education has fluctuated.

The proportion of part-time students who don't continue with their first degree beyond the second year of study has fluctuated in the under-30 age group, and stayed roughly similar for the over-30 age group.

Projections on continuing with higher education show a similar trend.

HESA also makes projections about the proportion of students it thinks will leave with a degree, and the proportion it thinks will leave higher education without gaining any kind of qualification or having transferred elsewhere.

This means we can have a rough idea of the full 'drop-out' rate – taking account of students leaving in their second, third, or later years of study.

It projects that for those starting in 2014/15, 10.3% across the UK will leave without a qualification or a transfer. This proportion has remained relatively similar over the last three years and has been generally declining over the last 20 years.

A similar trend can generally be seen across all the individual countries of the UK.

Conclusion

The proportion of young UK students from disadvantaged areas dropping out of higher education in England by their second year is at its highest level for five years, but it's not a record high. That's looking at full-time students on their first degree, and is based on educational disadvantage. Disadvantaged students, including working-class students, are generally more likely to drop out than advantaged.

9 July 2017

⇨ The above information is reprinted with kind permission from Full Fact. Please visit www.fullfact.org for further information.

We need to talk about the mental health crisis in our universities

By Tom Mitchell

For years, a blind-spot in the British education system has been 'freshers' week'. Just at the synapse between parental supervision and apparent self-sufficiency, 18-year-olds across the country are confronted with seven days of barely-disguised debauchery and promiscuity, egged on by students' unions and JCRs.

Slowly but surely, the battle to confront this damaging and expensive 'tradition' is being won, with a survey conducted by headmasters last year finding that the number of sixth-formers who dreaded this organised bacchanal at least matched the number who revelled in it. As a result, instead of the expectation to hook-up with someone regrettable in your first week, most universities now offer 'quiet-night' alternatives for those who want to go to their first lecture with their bank account and honour intact.

However, the problem extends far beyond the first week. The number of students with mental health problems at university has risen to a record level, with 15,395 students disclosing their mental health issues in their first year – a fivefold increase in a decade. The number of dropouts caused by mental health difficulties more than quadrupled over a similar period. Liberal Democrat MP Norman Lamb said this represented "a crisis on campus with respect to students" mental health.'

Anecdotal experience suggests that Lamb's analysis is not far from the mark. A friend of mine was in an accommodation block where a minimum of six students out of 20 experienced mental health issues at some point during their first year, three of those were visibly self-harming and one was potentially suicidal. Given that all of those six were girls, the likelihood that there were boys who experienced similar difficulties but didn't talk about it is high.

Often, the onus falls on fellow students (who have no experience in handling such issues) to deal with depressive incidents. Given that new data shows 134 students in 2015 committed suicide, the pressure on friends of those struggling with depression or similar illnesses is immense, damaging their own studies and experience at university.

Something needs to change. But what?

First, the UK must also do something to address its drinking culture. Alcohol is a depressant, and often is an aggravating factor in cases of self-harm. In a comparison of drinking cultures, *The Guardian* found that in France "people drink extensively and steadily, but in small units". Parents drink with their children from a young age, meaning there is no tendency to binge the minute they've left their parents' supervision.

Meanwhile, in Britain, "drinking yourself insensible is not only acceptable, it is admired". *The Independent* reported that 'introducing drink within 'controlled environments' – such as the home – could be considered as 'advantageous' due to young people trying it within that controlled environment." One of the aims in doing this is so that, when students hit the legal age, excessive consumption won't occur as it won't be seen as a 'big deal'.

Secondly, we should attempt to curb the obsession with treating university as the moment to 'fly the nest'. The consequence of this attitude is that students are thrown into a new environment often hundreds of miles from their parents and support network. The reality is that the university experience of scraping a 2:1 coupled with unlimited drinking doesn't mature students; real independence stems from earning your own salary and paying for your own things.

Given that most graduates will move back into the family home for a period after university, it shouldn't be seen as a pre-requisite to study somewhere miles from where you grew up. For many students on the continent, going to university close to home is the expectation. If this attitude was replicated here, then students who aren't yet ready to live independently would be more likely to swim than sink.

On a practical level, there must be a concerted effort to improve the pastoral care offered by universities. Too often there are cases of mental health officers being alerted to issues and failing to follow them up. Data from *The Guardian* shows that some universities are cutting back on the number of counsellors they employ, or are not recruiting more to meet the rise in demand. The University of Stirling, for example, reduced numbers from 2.44 full-time equivalent (fte) staff four years ago to 1.4 fte this year. This comes despite a 68% increase in demand.

As things stand, universities are seething with people who either have mental health issues, or are caring for those with such problems. This is a situation that needs to be urgently addressed. The success in improving the freshers' week experience should give us the hope and the impetus that a wider reform of attitudes and expectations can subject fewer young people to the turmoil of a mental health crisis.

6 September 2017

⇨ The above information is reprinted with kind permission from Backbench. Please visit www.bbench.co.uk for further information.

© 2018 Backbench

About student mental health

By Nicola Bryom, founder and trustee of Student Minds

Student Minds is the UK's student mental health charity, providing information about student mental health and local peer support programmes.

Studying is likely to bring a number of changes to your life. Hopefully it should be enjoyable and interesting, but it can also be challenging – especially if you're also living with a mental health problem. You might face challenges such as:

⇨ meeting and working with new people

⇨ exams, deadlines for written work or presentations

⇨ managing your own finances

⇨ coping with homesickness

⇨ balancing the demands of studying with other commitments

⇨ maintaining relationships with family and old friends

⇨ leaving home, finding new housing and living with new people.

Coping with new challenges can have an impact on your mental health, but there are lots of things that you can do to make your time as a student easier and more enjoyable.

The tutors who I chose to open up to were supportive. It was as a result of asking for help that I realised that with a few adjustments I would be able to finish my course, and nobody thought any less of me.

Students are also at somewhat higher risk of developing mental health problems. This could be because of:

⇨ Your age – many students are young people, and for many people this is the age when you first develop a mental health problem.

⇨ Stress – becoming a student can be a stressful experience. Although stress isn't a mental health problem, it can lead to mental health problems like depression and anxiety.

⇨ Lack of support – you might have left home for the first time, or just don't have enough time to see your friends and family. Not having a good support network can make you vulnerable to developing a mental health problem.

⇨ The above information is reprinted with kind permission from Mind. Please visit www.mind.org.uk for further information.

© 2018 Mind

Confronting my social anxiety at university

Max, a volunteer at Mind Cymru, shares his experience of social anxiety and how he is overcoming this.

Coming to university was a lot harder than I expected. It was a whole new experience in a city I had never been to before. I have always been a shy person. In an environment where many of my peers were quite loud and outgoing I quickly felt lonely, overwhelmed and, at times, quite depressed due to my social skills, or lack thereof.

Because of my difficulty socialising, my relationship with my flatmates in university halls was at first quite strained. I wanted to be good friends with them but my general anxiety had a big impact on how I attempted to do so.

The strain of all this had an effect on my university work. I became more and more stressed and found it increasingly hard to concentrate.

I knew I had to do something, so I went to my student services. They got my GP to refer me to speech and language therapy at Cardiff's Heath Hospital. This was the beginning of a positive and ongoing process to develop greater confidence in my communication and social skills. I was increasingly outgoing, going to parties and becoming more comfortable within other similar social situations. I also made new and valued friends.

Another situation where my social anxiety was particularly challenging was giving presentations at university, either by myself or with others. Very often, I knew quite clearly what I wanted to say, but the words just didn't want to come out. With the help of speech and language therapy and a bit of practice this got a little better. Indeed, when I gave presentations as part of the Graduate Academy, feedback suggested it had improved quite a bit. Without the support I received and the improvement in my social confidence as a result of this, I might not even have attended the Graduate Academy or involved myself in the Prince's Trust.

Though I am still a relatively shy person I have also been told by many people how equally determined I am. Despite my personal challenges, I am intent on not letting this be a barrier to me in my future life or my career. Although my strength lies with my written communication skills I am extremely eager to develop and strengthen my verbal skills, in part with the help of Mind Cymru, where I volunteer.

One of the ways I am challenging myself to increase my confidence is by taking on reception duties while being supported and learning with another volunteer. Through simply saying hello and interacting with visitors I am developing my confidence to strike up a quick and friendly conversation. This might not seem like a big deal to some people, but it's a great achievement for me.

While volunteering at Mind I have built good working relationships with my colleagues and I am confident I could do so again in my future career. And I know I can develop my abilities and confidence further for other situations like interviews, which I have found hard before.

In the end I am glad I shared my worries during university. With the help of the many good friends I have made here, including as a volunteer at Mind and SNAP Cymru, I have come to love Cardiff. I am proud of how far I've come and I am positive I can make even more progress.

Max Dean

Students who do nothing but study may struggle to get a job

THE CONVERSATION

An article from **The Conversation.**

By Pathik Pathak, Faculty Director of Social Entrepreneurship, Founding Director of Social Impact Lab, University of Southampton

Ernst and Young was the first prominent graduate employer to decide that its own entry criteria were a more accurate judge of job applicants than the degree classifications on their CVs. But similar moves away from a reliance on degree grades are now taking root at other big accountancy firms PwC and Deloitte, too.

The latest Global Employability University Survey, published in November 2015, reinforces the message that employers are placing a lower value on degree grades. But the survey also appears to suggest that extracurricular activities are equally lowly regarded, with just 10%

of European employers citing this as a criteria they use to make recruitment decisions.

These results appear to contradict the findings of our ongoing research into the motivations behind the growth of social entrepreneurship – broadly defined as the act of blending social missions with innovative business practice, among university students in the UK.

As part of our ongoing research we have asked 150 students across the UK who were taking part in extra-curricular social entrepreneurship to reflect on their experiences. They believed that these activities were not only complementing their degree

programmes, but were even more valuable for their future employability than their degree programmes.

The right skills mix

Yet the most important criteria employers use for recruitment decisions, according to the Global Employability University Survey, is the skills profile of applicants. Over half of all European employers cited specific skills, including innovation, leadership, networking and design skills, as the most important factor in their recruitment decisions.

Over recent years, societies such as Enactus, the global social enterprise organisation, has grown exponentially, with several university societies, such as those at my own university, Southampton, but also at Sheffield and Nottingham, doubling or tripling membership over a five-year period.

We've also seen the rise of social impact societies such as Student Hubs, which offer volunteering and placement opportunities in local communities, as well as more subject-specific organisations such as Engineers Without Borders.

Some of the growth of these societies should certainly be attributed to the rise of social and environmental consciousness among students, but there's also emerging evidence of

students making strategic decisions about how to use their free time outside formal teaching. Students are starting to discern between extracurricular activities which boost their employability – usually by developing soft skills or exposing them to new networks – and those that don't.

Such decisions are informed by the close relationship that some student societies have started to enjoy with corporate employers, such as KPMG, Deloitte, Waitrose and Barclays. Society alumni who have gone on to work for top-level graduate employers also feed their experiences back to university students.

The kinds of skills cultivated through social entrepreneurship are linked to the soft skills that graduate employers have repeatedly told us they prize, but which they believe graduates lack. Chief among these are creativity, resourcefulness, team-working, resilience, IT skills, and innovation. They are also the skills which will future-proof graduates against the changing nature of skilled work.

Entrepreneurial extracurricular activities also offer students the opportunity to develop their professional networks. In an age in which 'the post and pray' method of sending off CVs to find work is obsolete, adeptly mobilising networks is as critical as being able to demonstrate relevant knowledge and skills.

Give students a helping hand

As the importance of skills over qualifications grows for employers when they make recruitment decisions, there will be a greater need to properly distinguish between employment and employability. Employability cannot and should not be reduced to measuring how many graduates are employed. It should be understood as a blend of knowledge, skills and social capital, with employment a desired outcome but not the ultimate benchmark. Universities should not be content simply to offer students a leg up to their first job, but must set them up for careers that they value, and for resilience and flexibility in a volatile graduate labour market.

Unfortunately, league tables of universities continue to privilege short-term employment data, ranking institutions on how many graduates have a job after six months, instead of looking at the skills they develop that could help them further into their careers.

Our ongoing research indicates that students are seeking out opportunities to grow their skills and social capital through extra-curricular activities.

Often, it is a self-selecting few who corral the best opportunities. Even among those who do, many struggle to articulate the skills developed outside the formal higher education experience – explaining why extra-curricular activities are accorded such little significance by European employers.

To level the playing field, universities should be making the development of soft skills and network building a part of the curriculum. There are non-invasive, light-touch ways of doing this which might only require gentle tweaks to degree programmes and not place too great a burden on academics.

At the same time, the message shouldn't be that business as usual will suffice – it is incumbent upon universities to take the issue of employability seriously, and not leave it as an afterthought.

9 February 2016

⇨ The above information is reprinted with kind permission from *The Conversation*. Please visit www.theconversation.com for further information.

Most graduates will never pay off their student loans

THE CONVERSATION

***An article from* The Conversation.**

By Andrew Gunn, Researcher in Higher Education Policy, University of Leeds

New findings show that more than 70% of students who left university last year are never expected to finish repaying their loans. The report by the Institute for Fiscal Studies (IFS) shows that many of these graduates – the first cohort to pay the higher £9,000 fees – will be making repayments for 30 years. This means that a large number of graduates will be paying back their loans well into their 50s – and a growing proportion of the money lent out will never be repaid.

This is because, under the current system in England, when graduates earn over £21,000 they start making repayments of 9% of their salary above that threshold. And if the loan isn't repaid within 30 years, the outstanding balance is written off.

These new findings add to concerns the current policy of lending large sums to students to pay for their degree – rather than funding universities directly – is not sustainable over the long term. There have been calls by members of the Conservative party for a rethink over fees policy – and some have suggested that the end of tuition fees could be on the horizon.

The political debate

Student fees were already back on the agenda as a result of the recent election after Labour took the lion's share of student votes with their promise of wiping out tuition fees altogether.

Analysis by YouGov has also shown that the electorate is deeply divided by age and level of education: younger and more educated people were found to be less likely to vote Conservative. Understandably, the Conservative party is now concerned it could cost them an election in future.

This has led to Damien Green, the first secretary of state – and effectively Theresa May's deputy – saying that a "national debate2 on student fees may be needed. Green also added that the Conservatives will have to "change hard" to entice young educated voters away from Labour.

In response, universities minister Jo Johnson is doubling down on current policy, arguing disadvantaged young people are now 43% more likely to go to university than in 2010 and that abolishing tuition fees would cost taxpayers an additional £100 billion

by 2025. He also points to the fact that many loans are not fully repaid, which he argues shows the Government is subsiding the lowest-earning graduates.

The realities of fees and funding

What Johnson says is correct, there has been a big increase in the number of disadvantaged students going to university. But one of the main reasons for this is because at the same time as increasing fees, the Government also sought to remove the 'cap' on student numbers – so there is no longer a limit to the total number of places on offer.

Prior to the cap being removed in England, undergraduate education was paid for through taxes – as is still the case in Scotland – meaning the number of places had to be capped because the Government only has so much money to spend.

So removing the cap in England has enabled universities to make more offers to young people from disadvantaged backgrounds. This has been mainly through 'contextual admissions' – which is

where information including school performance data and socioeconomic markers are used to provide background to an application.

Indebted graduates

The proportion of young people entering undergraduate education has grown massively over time (student numbers have almost doubled since 1992) meaning those educated at university are no longer considered to be an 'elite' group. In real terms this means that, as a group of voters, the student population expands every year – making them more influential. This is not just an electorate with more graduates, but one with more indebted graduates.

Last year maintenance grants were replaced with maintenance loans – which has increased student borrowing further. And, as the IFS report shows, this decision means students from the poorest backgrounds will now have debts of on average £57,000 after a three-year degree – as these students will need to take out the maximum loan amount.

Then there is also the issue of the interest rate charged on the loans and how much graduates earn before they start paying it back. In recent years students have taken on ever-larger loans – and this, combined

with rising interest rates, is making it more expensive for graduates and undermining confidence in the system. As the IFS reports, this has hit poorer students and middle-earning graduates the hardest.

Despite this, the policy on fees isn't about to change just yet. The Conservatives are currently occupied with dealing with consequences of some of their more unpopular policies – such as abandoning the creation of new grammar schools and considering what to do with their proposals for technical education.

But sooner or later the Conservatives will need to produce another

manifesto. And the current debate, along with lessons learnt from the last election, may mean they revise their electoral offer to students and graduates – as all political parties look to adjust to this new electoral reality.

7 July 2017

⇨ The above information is reprinted with kind permission from *The Conversation*. Please visit www. theconversation.com for further information.

Gap between graduate and non-graduate wages "shows signs of waning"

IFS says substantial difference in earnings is likely to decrease in future as more people pursue higher education.

By Sally Weale and Richard Adams

University graduates continue to enjoy higher earnings than their non-graduate peers, but there are signs the gap may soon shrink, according to the Institute for Fiscal Studies (IFS).

The IFS publishes its results as hundreds of thousands of teenagers receive their A-level results. Record

numbers will make the decision to go to university, which in England means accruing significant debt as a result of the annual £9,000 tuition fees.

Despite concern that a dramatic increase in the number of young people going to university has led to a decline in graduate wages relative to those of school-leavers, the IFS says

the graduate premium has remained the same for two decades. It says, however, that further increases in graduate numbers could start to erode the premium. "It's just that the gain might be smaller in the future than it is now," the report notes, adding that going to university will probably remain worthwhile.

The increasing cost of going to university was flagged up again on Wednesday when it emerged that Exeter University plans to raise tuition fees to £9,250 for existing students, rather than just new students. Some universities have chosen to apply the fee increase only to new students beginning their studies in 2017.

The shadow higher education spokesman, Gorden Marsden, accused Exeter of moving the goal posts. "Students have signed up, largely for three-year courses, on the assumption that changes in that time will not affect them."

The Government has long argued that the cost of going to university is more than justified by higher graduate earnings, but recent studies have suggested the value of a degree has declined because the supply of graduates has outstripped demand.

In 1993, only 13% of 25- to 29-year-olds had a first or higher degree. By 2015 the figure had tripled to 41%, and following the removal of the student numbers cap in 2015, graduate numbers are expected to increase further.

According to the IFS, median wages for both graduates and non-graduates fell by 15% between 2008 and 2015, but the wage difference between graduates and school-leavers has stayed at about 35% for the past two decades.

The main reason for the continuing graduate wage premium, the IFS said, was that firms had created more graduate jobs by hiring more managers and switching to less hierarchical structures. "This process cannot go on forever," it said. "There are now signs that it might be reaching a natural end, with some small falls in the wages of graduates in the private sector relative to school leavers in the most recent years. Further increases in the number of graduates could start to erode the graduate wage premium in the future."

The IFS researchers said they were puzzled that the rapid expansion in higher education numbers in recent years had not caused the 20% drop in the graduate wage premium their models predicted. Instead, they found that the labour market had changed to increase the proportion of staff working in management, as well as allowing workers more autonomy overall.

"While we do not claim that our empirical results for the organisational change explanation are definitive, we believe that they do provide a coherent explanation for the remarkable stability of the education wage differential from the early 1990s until the mid-2000s in the UK that occurred despite unprecedented increases in the share of entry workers with degree level education over the same period.

"This points to the UK responding to the substantial increase in university education through an adjustment in the organisational structure of work," the IFS concluded.

It said increasing numbers of future graduates "would result in declines in the education wage differential2 once the trend of hiring extra graduates into management had run its course. "There is already some sign of this decline in the private sector. The wage differential, though, remains substantial," it said.

The numbers of school leavers is likely to remain flat for a further four years, but university remains an increasingly popular option, with universities making strenuous efforts to recruit among the static pool of potential students. As a result, the next few years are likely to be a 'buyer's market' for those going to university, with universities making more generous offers in terms of grades required. A new report by the Social Market Foundation (SMF) found that the number of students from disadvantaged backgrounds going to university was increasing fast, especially those entering with vocational qualifications such as BTecs rather than A-levels.

Between 2008 and 2015, students entering higher education from the most disadvantaged backgrounds just with A-levels increased by 19%, while the research shows that those with BTecs increased by 116%.

"Large differences in entry rates exist between areas for young people with A-levels, but entry rates for those with BTecs or a combination of BTecs and A-levels are much more equal across areas [of the UK]," the report said.

The rise in the number of university students from disadvantaged areas has continued despite the increase in tuition fees. A student on a three-year undergraduate course who takes out a full maintenance loan will graduate with more than £50,000 of debt.

Students with vocational qualifications still struggle to get into the leading universities, though the SMF found some notable exceptions. King's College London nearly quadrupled the number of young people with BTecs it took in between 2008 and 2015, so that students with BTecs now make up more than 7% of its intake.

The SMF also found that graduates with a BTec and a degree have an hourly earnings premium of 20% compared with those with only a BTec as their highest qualification.

18 August 2016

⇨ The above information is reprinted with kind permission from *The Guardian*. Please visit www.theguardian.com for further information.

Key facts

- Berlin has been named as the top European university city for British students abroad (page 2)

- Higher education continues to be a popular option despite the rise in tuition fees, with an all-time high of 241,585 18-year-olds across the UK accepted onto degree courses in 2017. (page 3)

- Since 2014, 56,200 workers have enrolled on higher and degree apprenticeships, studying a range of qualifications from foundation degree level to full Masters. (page 3)

- Studying for a degree will cost you £9,000 per year in tuition fees, plus additional living expenses. It's estimated that an undergraduate could leave university with up to £50,000 worth of debt. However you won't start repayments until you earn a minimum of £21,000 a year. (page 3)

- Between 2010 and 2016 there was a 5.5 per cent increase in undergraduate numbers despite a decline in the number of 18-year-olds. (page 9)

- In 2012, the Government raised the maximum cost of university tuition fees from £3,000 to £9,000 a year, and that has since risen to £9,250. (page 10)

- The number of 18-year-olds entering higher education has risen in every year since 2012, whilst the number of people aged 20 and over has dropped off since 2015. (page 10)

- A higher level of 18-year-olds from the most disadvantaged areas are in higher education than ever before – 20% of that group entered higher education in 2017, compared to 15% in 2012, and 11% in 2006. (page 10)

- The number of part-time students in England declined by 51 per cent between 2010 and 2015 – and researchers say part of the fall was caused by higher tuition fees in 2012. (page 12)

- In April 2017, the Government is introducing an 'apprenticeship levy' (a 0.5% tax on an employer's paybill above £3 million per year), which is estimated to raise £2.8 billion in 2019–20. (page 13)

- The number of unconditional offers received by 18-year-olds from England, Northern Ireland and Wales rose by 40 per cent in a year – from 36,825 in 2016 to 51,615 in 2017. (page 15)

- Since 1998, tuition fees have progressively risen. In 2006, under the Labour Government, the Higher Education Act 2004 trebled fees to £3,000 per year and introduced deferred variable fees and tuition fee loans which are repaid after graduation. (page 18)

- Recent HESA figures show more than 328,000 students in the UK elected to remain in the family home last year. But with living costs on the rise and monthly rent in London now at a whopping average cost of £1,508 per month, it hardly comes as a surprise. (page 24)

- There were 238,900 18-year-olds in the UK accepted onto a full-time university course in 2016, the most ever recorded. This made up around half of all acceptances via UCAS that year. (page 25)

- Around 33% of all 18-year-olds in England were accepted into a university place in 2016 – the highest level recorded. In Wales it was around 30%, again the highest on record. (page 25)

- Entry rates for 18-year-olds in Northern Ireland rose to 35% in the year to 2016, the same level as 2014. (page 25)

- In 2016, the entry rate for 18-year-olds living in the most disadvantaged areas increased for all countries in the UK. It increased to the highest on record in England (almost 20%) and Wales (18%). In Northern Ireland it was at 16%, the second highest recorded level. (page 26)

- The entry rate to university of 18-year-old state school pupils in receipt of free school meals was also at a record high in 2016 – at about 16%. That's compared to almost 33% for those who didn't receive free school meals. (page 26)

- In the period March to May 1992, there were 984,000 people aged 18 to 24 in full-time education. In May to July 2016, there were 1.87 million, approximately one in every three people, aged 18 to 24 in full-time education. (page 27)

- The aged 18 to 24 population in Oxford and Cambridge increases by over 80% during university term-time. (page 28)

- Over a quarter of immigrants come to the UK for formal study. In 1977, there were 29,000 international students, rising to a peak of over eight times this amount in 2010. However, recent years have seen a decline in long-term immigrants arriving to study, with numbers falling to 164,000 in the year ending March 2016. (page 28)

- 8.8% of young students from the most disadvantaged fifth of areas undertaking their first full-time course left higher education after their first year in 2014/15. That's the highest level since 2009/10, when it was 9.3%. (page 30)

- The proportion of students under the age of 21 not continuing in higher education in the UK in their second year of study was 6.2% in 2014/15

  - It was highest for students at universities in Scotland (6.5%) and lowest in Northern Ireland (5.3%). (page 31)

- In 1993, only 13% of 25- to 29-year-olds had a first or higher degree. By 2015 the figure had tripled to 41%, and following the removal of the student numbers cap in 2015, graduate numbers are expected to increase further. (page 39)

A-levels

These are qualifications usually taken by students aged 16 to 18 at schools and sixth-form colleges, although they can be taken at any time by school leavers at local colleges or through distance learning. They provide an accepted route to degree courses and university and usually take two years to complete.

Apprenticeship

A form of vocational training which involves learning a trade or skill through working. An apprentice will often shadow an experienced practitioner of a trade, learning the occupation 'on the job'. Some apprenticeships can take many years.

Career College

Career Colleges are schools designed to provide vocational education. This means that students will learn and develop skills necessary to perform particular jobs.

Degree

An honours degree is the most common qualification awarded on graduation from university. It is graded according to classification: first class (a 'first'), upper second class (2:1), lower second class (2:2), third class (a 'third') and fail.

Further education

Education for 16 to 18-year-olds, for example college or sixth form.

Gap year

A year away from study or full-time employment, usually taken before starting university or after graduating. Gap years can help students to broaden their horizons through travel or volunteering.

Graduate

Someone who has studied for and been awarded a degree.

Halls of residence

Most new students live in accommodation provided by the university, called halls of residence.

Higher education

Post-18 education, usually provided by a university and leading to the award of a degree or postgraduate qualification. There are currently over two million higher education students in the UK.

Postgraduate

A postgraduate is a student who has completed a degree and gone on to further academic study, such as a PhD or a Masters course.

State school

A school which is funded and run by the Government, at no cost to the pupils. An independent school, on the other hand, is one which is privately run and which pupils pay a fee to attend. These are sometimes known as 'private schools' or 'public schools' (please note, not all private schools are public schools).

Student debt

A higher education student can apply for a student loan from the Government, which they begin paying back monthly after graduation once they are earning a certain salary. They may also incur additional debts such as overdrafts while at university.

Student loan

A sum of money leant to students by the Government in order to pay for their tuition and maintenance fees. Is paid back gradually once the graduate is earning over £21,000 per year.

Undergraduate

An undergraduate is a term applied to a student studying towards a first degree but who has not yet graduated.

Vocational

A qualification which is relevant to a particular career and can be expected to provide a route into that career.

Assignments

Brainstorming

Brainstorm what you know about student life.

What is a graduate?

What is an apprenticeship?

What is a bursary?

What do you understand by the term 'night owl'?

Research

⇨ Conduct a survey amongst your class mates. How many of them are considering going to university? How many would choose to still live at home when they do? Consider the percentages of boys versus girls who prefer to stay at home. Think of at least six questions to ask them and produce a chart to show your findings.

⇨ In small groups, do some research into different universities in the UK. What are the differences in the different types of course each one offers? Write a report on your findings and share with your class.

⇨ Do some research into student loans. Who is most likely to be entitled to a loan? How do you apply for a student loan? How much would you receive? How and when would you pay it back? Write a report which should cover one A4 side and share with the rest of your class.

⇨ In pairs, do some research into apprenticeships in the UK. You should consider the types of apprenticeships on offer, the benefits they offer and the pay apprentices might receive. How long might an apprenticeship last? Write a short report on your findings.

⇨ Visit a local bookshop and find out how many books there are giving information and advice about universities. Do you feel the books you come across are helpful and give the advice needed? Make some notes on your findings and share with the rest of your class.

Design

⇨ Imagine you work for a university and have been asked to design a poster to advertise its facilities. It should inform students what it has to offer and encourage them to apply for a place there. Tell them why your university is the one to go for.

⇨ Produce a leaflet about student loans. It should provide as much information as possible, including how to apply for a loan.

⇨ In pairs, design a leaflet which would help students to budget. Your leaflet should give practical advice on how students can manage their money.

⇨ Choose an article from this book and design an illustration highlighting its key points.

Oral

⇨ In pairs, one of you should play the role of a student who wants to go to university and the other one should try to persuade them that an apprenticeship would be better. Then reverse roles.

⇨ Read the article on page 21, *Night owl students perform worse academically due to 'social jet lag'*. Discuss this statement in small groups and feedback to the rest of the class.

⇨ In pairs, go through this book and discuss the cartoons you come across. Think about what the artist was trying to portray with each illustration.

⇨ Read the article on page 24 *More students choosing to live at home and commute*. As a class, discuss this statement.

⇨ Interview your parents and teachers. Find out how many of them went to university. How many of them went straight out to work? Ask them the reasons they made the choices they made. Write some notes on your findings and feedback to the rest of the class.

Reading/writing

⇨ Write a one-paragraph definition of the word 'university' and then compare it with a classmate's.

⇨ Write a one-paragraph definition of the word 'apprenticeship' and then compare it with a classmate's.

⇨ Imagine you are an Agony Aunt/Uncle and have received a letter from a young boy saying his parents are pressurising him to go to university. He does not want to go but feels if he does not he will let them down. Write a suitable reply.

⇨ Read the article on page 32 *We need to talk about the mental health crisis in our universities*. Write a blog post highlighting this issue and giving advice as to where students can go for help if they are suffering from mental health issues.

⇨ Read the book *Porterhouse Blue* by Tom Sharp, a satirical look at Cambridge University life and the struggle between tradition and reform. Write a review of the book which should cover at least two A4 sides.

Acknowledgements

The publisher is grateful for permission to reproduce the material in this book. While every care has been taken to trace and acknowledge copyright, the publisher tenders its apology for any accidental infringement or where copyright has proved untraceable. The publisher would be pleased to come to a suitable arrangement in any such case with the rightful owner.

Images

All images courtesy of iStock except pages 21 and 29: Jackie Staines, and pages 24 and 28 Morguefile

Illustrations

Don Hatcher: pages 6 & 31. Simon Kneebone: pages 23 & 37. Angelo Madrid: pages 15 & 36.

Additional acknowledgements

With thanks to the Independence team: Shelley Baldry, Danielle Lobban, Jackie Staines and Jan Sunderland.

Tina Brand

Cambridge, June 2018